STEP BY STEP

A PRIMER ON "THE ESTABLISHMENT" DESTRUCTION OF AMERICAN DEMOCRACY AND SOVEREIGNTY IN PURSUIT OF A "NEW INTERNATIONAL ECONOMIC ORDER" OR "NEW WORLD ORDER" AT THE EXPENSE OF AMERICANS

Donn W. Fletcher

ISBN 10: 1724719122
ISBN 13: 9781724719126
Library of Congress Control Number: 2018909187

*This book is dedicated to
Americans who understand
working and producing,
not giving and taking,
made America the greatest
country in the world, and
hopefully are intelligent
enough not to elect another
member of the America
destroying "Establishment."*

CONTENTS

PREFACE

At the beginning of the Twenty First Century, working, producing, taxpaying, asset holding Americans desiring to maintain the faith, culture and values of those who gave birth to America, nurtured and guided it, and gave their lives for it for over two hundred years are under attack.

They are under attack by radical members of the Islamic faith who desire to displace American culture and laws with Islamic culture and laws that proactively prohibit freedom of religion, persecute and even sentence to death many whose lifestyles or beliefs are inconsistent with Islam that provides only hopelessness and poverty to the vast majority of its adherents.

They are under attack by hordes of illegal immigrants from Mexico, a country with a different culture whose leaders have stated a desire to regain a large part of America's geography, and displace its culture with their own that has also provided only poverty and hopelessness to over forty percent of its citizens.

They are also under attack by elected members of their own Government who mount wars against concepts they know cannot be defeated while, for the sake of political correctness, refuse to specifically identify the actual enemies they withhold truths about, while allying with others who satisfy their criteria for enemies.

These members of their Government function solely for the benefit of themselves and other members of their America destroying so-called *"elite"* who should only be referred to as the *"effete elite"* because they are so feeble in their conduct, refusing to uphold their sworn duties to provide for the safety of Americans, protect their borders or maintain their Constitutional protections, but have chosen instead, through several administrations of both parties, to support only the interests of others whose objective is to deprive Americans of their culture, freedom, right of self-determination and prosperity.

They are also under attack by these members of their government through their "education" system that is, in reality, an indoctrination system not unlike those in totalitarian societies in Asia and Europe in the first half of the twentieth century.

This was, as planned, ensuring a hopeless future for America by indoctrinating its youth with what to think, rather than how to

2

think, and depriving them of knowledge of the faith, culture, and values that produced the freest and most prosperous society in the history of humankind... all for the monetary and power benefit of the most powerful one percent in their quixotic desire for an homogenized, open borders world under one central government, or as George H.W. Bush declared in 1989; a *"New World Order."*

Beginning in the weeks after Donald J. Trump began his campaign for the forty-fifth Presidency we were witness to the success of this system, as ignorant, indoctrinated youth and members of the prior indoctrinated generation took to the streets, under the guidance of also indoctrinated "education" faculties, in violent protests of ignorance against the common sense proposals of candidate Trump to protect them, their county and future by diverting it off its planned course of failure as a free and sovereign nation that was begun in earnest in 1973.

This work is a non-partisan presentation of truths about this and their Government to working, producing, taxpaying, asset holding, and any other Americans who desire to retake control of their country from *"the Establishment"* that entirely for the benefit of its members and their anti-American values constituencies are working against the interests of Americans and their country, ensuring its economic and cultural demise if its course is not diverted as Trump is hoping to be able to do for the benefit of all Americans.

It is not intended to be a pleasurable read. It is intended to be an educational one to instill a necessary sense of urgency to cause the dialogue to become meaningful by recognizing the reality of America's situation, and injecting the common sense required to accomplish Trump's objectives for the benefit of all of us.

Hopefully, the contents herein will help provide a spark of initiative to a sufficient number of Americans to cause them to recognize a President Trump would be our last chance to recover the America that was, and embrace his efforts to assiduously pursue regaining the faith, culture and values that made America great... before it is too late.

PROLOGUE

As stated on the cover; this book it is "a primer," a simple book providing the first principles of a subject. So with that in mind let's begin with a simple fact that seems to be eluding the minds of those discussing the state of affairs of America at the beginning of the 21st Century.

***"First we have to know we have a problem then recognize
what the problem is before we can solve it."***

But no one ever addresses what the problem is. Deliberately we must conclude, although the reason is also elusive because it should be known to all those in politics and the media discussing it twenty-four seven.

That problem is not Russia, *"the left, Democrats, Liberals, the Deep State"* or any of the other superficialities occupying one hundred percent of the time wasted in these discussions.

The problem is the Internal Threat to the survival of the United States of America posed by *"the Establishment"* in control of the Government and most of the media for four decades as of 2018 under the direction of the relatively unknown mentor and puppeteer of five of the six Presidents preceding President Trump, as well as Hillary Clinton. That threat was Zbigniew Brzezinski, but even after his death the threat continues.

This is proven by Brzezinski's own words taken from his writings and comments presented in this book, including, in part: 1.) <u>reducing through immigration the political power of the Eurocentric electorate</u> that created America, and 2<u>.) reducing American prosperity through trade deals and organizations to create *"equilibrium"* with other economies to create a *"New International Economic Order,"* i.e., *New World Order*</u>.

In other words: 1.) load America with a critical mass of uneducated Government dependent Third World immigrants sufficient to make them the majority population that when given the power to vote will empower the Government because of their dependency on it, and 2.) take capital investment, production and jobs out of America and move them to the Third World to endeavor to make it richer at the expense of reducing American wealth and prosperity.

Thus, endeavoring to do via worldwide communism that proven an abysmal failure many times in the 20th Century that is in contradiction to Winston Churchill's wise guidance on the subject: ***"You don't make the poor richer by making the rich poorer"***

Given this, most except millions of *"millennials"* deliberately indoctrinated with the tenets of communism for this purpose would see this academic egghead lunacy can lead nowhere but to massive American and worldwide economic regression and concomitant failure of nations as it did in the Soviet Union.

But if there would have ever been a *"Deep State,"* as we frequently hear, Brzezinski and his cabal of students and acolytes would have comprised it. However, there was never really a *"Deep State"* because all of those in power doing his bidding and continuing to pursue his America destroying plans are not *"Deep"* anything. They are all well-known, highly placed political whores, many of whom have been *"outed"* since Trump has arisen and they are publicly endeavoring to take him down.

Examples are: the Bush family dating back three generations in highly placed Government positions from which they have been engaged in various anti-American activities including lying to start unnecessary wars further impoverishing Americans, previous Presidents; Lyndon Johnson who did the same, Jimmy Carter who did much irreparable damage in education and immigration, Bill Clinton who did tremendous damage to American industry and wealth, and Obama who deliberately exacerbated all Carter did.

In addition to ex-Presidents are members of Congress, including John McCain who was on the ground in the Ukraine encouraging dissidents to overthrow the elected head of that country's government, Diane Feinstein who was a charter member of Brzezinski's group, and many others in Congress publicly endeavoring to derail Trump's bid for the Presidency to prevent him doing what the people wanted him to do.

Then there have been two Attorney Generals and Assistant A.G.s, plus two FBI Directors and a dozen other top Officials of that organization, the ex-Directors of the National Security Agency and the C.I.A., ninety percent of the press and oh so many more it is difficult to envision how America can be saved, let alone be made "*Great Again*." But if it can Trump is the one who will do it!

***

So, we now know the real problem needing to be solved if America is to be saved is how to dislodge all the *"the Establishment"* bought and paid for political whores so deeply embedded in the U.S. Government, media and big business it seems an insurmountable problem.

But it is not if a majority of Americans are made aware of this fact. The ballot box is the solution.

If a majority of non-swamp dwellers can continue to be elected and stay in control of Congress America can be saved. But it is a big, daunting task because the "swamp" is vast, deep and populated with many slimy creatures of long-term tenure.

The last example of their endurance was in the year 2000 when Alan Keys, a Republican Presidential Primaries Republican non-Establishment candidate stated even then regarding the state of America at the time: "*The house is burning down and no one is yelling, fire!*"

Americans who for at least two decades by that time were… as they still are two presidents later in 2016… too busy fiddling with sports, movies, music, celebrities and recreating to even be aware of what Mr. Keyes was really saying.

He was also shunned by many because he was not representative of the majority political voice of his race.

Even his chosen Republican Party shut him out of one of their primary debates though he was the most articulate of the candidates in stating what are supposed to be the values and ideals of his chosen party. Why?

Mr. Keyes, like Donald Trump sixteen years later in 2016, was not a member of "*the Establishment*," and what he was defending Republicans should have supported were the values that historically served as an example for the world by providing the most prosperous and free society humans have ever experienced.

But these values are inconsistent with those of the majority, controlling, "*Establishment*" members of his party because it, as most should have become aware by the middle of 2016 as a result of the conduct of the Republican Party leadership, is nothing but one of two veneers of "*the Establishment*" cabal actually in control of the U.S. Government.

The "two party" system is nothing but a thin veneer… a sham… created to appease, control and divide the electorate on the basis of its human herd instincts of needing to belong and have leadership lead them where it desires they be led.

This enables "*the Establishment*" to "*divide and conquer*" them to accomplish what is desired for the benefit of its membership that actually represents only about one percent of the population.

This is to the detriment of the other ninety-nine percent of an increasingly… by design… disparate electorate unaware of what is being done to them by and for the sole benefit of "*the Establishment*" that consists of owners and the owned, neither of which are bound by traditional values, ethics, morals, even laws as proven by the F.B.I. Director, and the Attorney General in July 2016. Nor are they working for the good of the nation and its citizens. M-O-N-E-Y is the sole driving force.

The owners are wealthy individuals, large, corporations, especially global ones, insurance, healthcare and pharmaceutical companies, defense contractors, big banks, and others who have money and favors to pay for what they desire.

The owned…"*bought and paid for*"… are those in positions of power or seeking these positions such as members of Congress, heads of Government agencies, even the Presidency, i.e., positions that control Government decisions, actions and legislation that can enhance the finances of the owners without regard for the people or finances and future of the country… and let's not forget the media that covers up, misleads, and tells outright lies to enable the growth of this destruction.

Thus, the pro-American agenda Mr. Keyes was advocating in 2000, and Donald Trump in 2016, is a threat to the entirety of "*the Establishment,*" and its money and power because the stated agenda of both candidates provided knowledge to the people, knowledge of what "*the Establishment*" has been doing, and how it has adversely affected Americans and their country, and if implemented would be the end of their money and power.

Additionally what both proposed is deemed politically incorrect, but not solely because of a conservative point of view. It is also deemed culturally improper because it threatens the *"divide and conquer"* for power element of *"the Establishment"* plans.

It is not acceptable to be a voice in favor of the opportunity afforded everyone by the culture and economic system *"the Establishment"* and its *"leftist, liberal progressive"* media despise so vehemently.

From the point of view of what passes for main stream minority culture in America <u>as represented by the media</u> advocating being educated, promoting the economic system, democracy, lack of dependency, families and marriage, rather than illegitimacy that are best for everyone is racist.

Thus, Mr. Keyes and others like he and Trump who achieved a degree of success in the American Capitalist System are called racist with the tacit approval of *"the Establishment"* since they have not been heard to speak out against this or promote the economic system that is the hope for the future of all Americans and everyone everywhere.

They are continuously working assiduously to convince minorities they are victims of a white, racist society that has deprived them of their fair share of America's economic success. Why?

Minorities, since the beginning of the last half of the Twentieth Century, have been convinced by *"the Establishment"* and their co-conspirators in the minority "leadership" they are victims, which they are. However, they are not victims of a white, racist society. They are victims of their own "leadership."

Minority "leadership," like all who desire to attain leadership positions of power, as opposed to working for the betterment of themselves and others through work, setting an example and helping others through their deeds, understands to be a leader it is necessary to have a constituency.

The easiest way to create a constituency is to define those you want to lead as different from, being deprived by, or mistreated by others you can target as an obstruction to your chosen constituency's ability to obtain their fair share of freedom, land, economic success, or opportunity. Then define yourself, through words and deeds, as one who can obtain for them that which you have convinced them is unattainable without your leadership.

This is defined as classic "*divide and conquer.*"

However, minority "leadership" is not solely responsible for this victimization of minorities in America. Self-defined *"liberal progressives"* or whatever members of this contingent of *"the Establishment,"* like Hillary Clinton, choose to call themselves are just as guilty, if not more so, in the victimization of certain people for political power. But this is not true of all "liberals."

There are two kinds of these *"liberals"* just as there are two kinds of communists, or those of other political or religious affiliations; those who follow without questioning or seeking answers and enlightenment, and those who seek positions of leadership and power by deliberately fostering attitudes, beliefs, conflicts, untruths, opinions, or whatever they perceive will provide them the position and power they desire.

It is the latter, Clintonesque, not the former, *"liberal progressives"* who share responsibility with minority "leadership," for victimization of minorities and the resultant denigration of American society in general through their agenda of multiculturalism, *"diversity"* and political correctness that is intended to impede any improvement in the declining state of American society by inhibiting open discussion of any of the topics it is absolutely necessary to discuss if solutions are to be found and implemented. Why?

Knowledge is power, but uncommon knowledge superior to that of those over whom one desires to have power and control provides even greater power. Also, the more fearful people are to openly discuss anything that could be disruptive to the power bases of those in power the less likely it is those who are subject to the desires of the powerful will be permitted the collective knowledge to enable them to mount any opposition to their power.

A divided population is much more susceptible to control by a strong central government and the self-interests of those in *"the Establishment"* whose desire is to use segments of the divided population as their power base than is a population unified in language, customs, desires, goals, and objectives.

Thus although short sighted, power is the answer. Strong central government power over a divided population, based upon their words, actions, deeds and legislation is the desire of *"leftist, liberal progressive"* Democrats and many Republican members of *"the Establishment"* whose plans are to ensure continuation of this.

Anyone who disagrees with the previous regarding *"the Establishment,"* minorities, their leadership, *"liberalism,"* political correctness, or any of the rest of it should consider the fact the foundation of upward mobility to a better and more prosperous life is knowledge gained primarily through education.

Although there are individual exceptions, there are not any examples wherein *"diversity"* of language, ethnicity, religion, culture, etc., promoted by *"the Establishment"* media as *"strength"* has resulted in harmonious coexistence of the various groups required for an effective education system. To the contrary; education in America has declined dramatically since creation of the Department of Education by President Carter when "teaching" what to think, not how, began.

Consider: why do *"liberal progressives"* and minority "leadership," like the Congressional Black Caucus and other Democrats send their offspring to private schools, rather than public "school" holding pens of Washington D.C., oppose opportunity for inner city, predominately black youth to attend better schools?

Are they afraid they might become better educated, more knowledgeable, and able to ascertain how badly they are disadvantaged by their "leadership" and other *"Establishment"* members who for their own power encourage disharmony throughout American society by continually promoting their racially divisive, *"diversity"* agenda to the detriment of all, especially minorities?

To have a relatively free and democratic society like America had before *"the Establishment"* obtained *de facto* control of its government in the 1970s it is necessary to have an educated, informed and knowledgeable population.

An educated, knowledgeable population, not an indoctrinated one as has been created through the Government "common core" program, would be much less susceptible to *"the Establishment"* lies and propaganda of persons and groups who use the population as a base for enhancement of personal power and wealth.

Would an educated minority population in possession of facts of upward mobility advantages of Western culture, education and knowledge available to them as Americans, rather than being "taught" ancestral heritage and *faux* benefits of *"diversity,"* engendered with a spirit of harmony and the benefits of collective interests be as accepting of the deliberately divisive lies of their "leadership" over the informed articulation of an Alan Keyes, Thomas Sowell, or Clarence Thomas?

Would Mexican Americans continue to vote for those of their own ethnicity and *"liberal progressives"* who promote bilingual education and cultural *"diversity"* if they were aware, as are the Chinese, Swiss, Dutch, and so many others, of the necessity of the English language for upward mobility and economic success on a worldwide basis, the divisiveness of *"diversity,"* and the fact children learn languages better at an early age?

The answer to these questions is, obviously, no. The reason: rarely do individuals choose that which is detrimental to them, or the future of their children.

Therefore, it would seem, since they have within their power the ability to educate, inform and help all Americans better their lot in life, and thus enhance America for everyone, non-*"Establishment,"* conservative Republicans, if there are any left, would aggressively attack programs and agenda of the *"liberal progressive,"* minority "leadership," and others working on their special interest power base programs, rather than pandering to them to the detriment of all Americans and the future of the nation.

***

Why do Republicans insist on referring to them as *"my good friend"* and rarely confront those whose ideas they should be diametrically opposing? Has *"the Establishment"* grown so large and all powerful it cannot be confronted?

This must be the case since it is exceedingly rare to see a Republican demonstrate any backbone for anything of importance to their base or the future of liberty and prosperity in America.

Maybe it is unfair to blame Republicans for their ineffectiveness. Maybe it is just a result of contemporary *"Establishment"* Republican culture in which anyone who does not toe the party line is not likely to last long in the party, achieve any success or even be supported by the party in the next election.

If one endeavors to do something to forestall all the gains of *"liberalism"* he or she would be out of step with *"the Establishment"* control of the party. After all, Republicans have provided Americans with two recent Presidents who demonstrated *"liberalism"* on the issues of illegal immigration and foreign trade that would make Bill Clinton proud, and could likely result in a President Hillary Clinton, due to Bush engendered "conservative" disaffection.

One would think so-called "conservative" Republicans would have naturally embraced Alan Keyes and Donald Trump who speak out and stand up for what Republicans historically represented, i.e., America. But, no! *"The Establishment"* agenda of *"diversity"* imposed via illegal immigration, political correctness to avoid truths being told, even trade deals favoring corporate America, and workers of other countries prevails over everything.

Proponents of true Republicanism have not been in control of the party since Ronald Reagan was succeeded by George Bush the First who was a *bona fide* member of *"the Establishment."*

He, after spending many *"Establishment"* Renaissance weekends at Hilton Head with Bill and Hillary Clinton and others who support the Brzezinski *"New International Economic Order"* One World Government to the detriment of America and all other sovereign nations... never covered by the press... apparently forgot he was not supposed to tell everyone about the *New World Order* he proclaimed after becoming President.

He also, like his son the second Bush President, demonstrated a strong affinity for ideals and leaders of other countries who do not have the best interests of America among their objectives, preeminent among them; the Saudi 'Royal' family.

In addition to these medieval tyrants who supplied sixteen of the hijackers on "9/11," and paid each of their families $250,000, the son seemed too close to the President of Mexico who was a strong supporter of illegal immigration of Mexican Nationals into the United States he referred to as *"natural migration."*

The son also proposed, *a la* Jimmy Carter, the first *New World Order* President, granting amnesty to millions of criminal, illegal aliens because, God help us, he either "thought" he was encouraging Latinos to vote for Republicans, or worse; he was fulfilling his obligations to *"the Establishment"* to continue implementing its *"diversity"* plans detrimental to working, taxpaying, asset owning Americans.

This he did, rather than fulfill his sworn, Constitutional obligation as President to protect America's borders from invasion, which he shirked in allying himself with the Mexican President at the expense of American taxpayers.

This illegal alien problem amounts to, as encouraged by his friend, then President Fox of Mexico, a deliberate foreign government encouraged invasion of sovereign American territory by over one million illegal invaders per year that are not, as the junior Bush stated, *"Just good folks looking for a better life."*

They are mostly members of Mexico's population that is the least educated and least productive who also, as a side benefit to Mexico's economy, send many of their U.S. earned dollars back to Mexico augmenting the tremendous benefits bestowed upon Mexico through NAFTA at the expense of the U.S. economy, by the elder Bush's *"New World Order"* weekend friends who preceded junior in the White House. It is, however, not in America's best interest.

It serves only the interests of Mexico, as does NAFTA that moved massive numbers of highly paying American jobs to Mexico to enhance U.S. auto maker's profits at the expense of the destruction of much of the American Middle Class.

In fact, NAFTA bestowed on Mexico so much massive new industrial might it created a new middle class there these illegal immigrants to the U.S. could be beneficiaries of, like hundreds of thousands, if not millions, of other Mexicans, if they were well enough educated or inclined to participate in Mexico's new booming, productive economy.

Aguascalientes, Mexico is like a new Detroit... only safer and better. Asian and European auto manufactures along with American makers are in evidence in a big way, and these massive industrial facilities are surrounded by sprawling subdivisions of middle class homes with new autos in the drives. Forbes called this "America's new car capital."

At another location in Mexico is another massive facility... probably a quarter mile long... where all of the kitchen appliances sold in America, except those made in Asia are manufactured.

No! Mexican illegal aliens in the U.S. are not "*Just good folks.*" They are poorly educated, economically disadvantaged, poor people from the back country farms and villages of third world Mexico where there is no welfare; food stamps, housing allowances, etc., and everyone has to work for his livelihood.

But, yes. They are coming to the U.S. "*looking for a better life*" solely because of these benefits provided at the monetary and jobs expense of Americans since Jimmy Carter and his *NWO "Establishment"* controllers deliberately implemented this *"divide and conquer"* step of the destruction of "America," as we knew it, by initiating the provision of welfare and other benefits for them.

But this was preceded by importation of the same socioeconomic level of large numbers from Vietnam and Cambodia in the 1960s under Democrat President Johnson, expanded by the second Bush with Somalis from Africa and others from the Middle East, and further accelerated by Obama who greatly expanded this *"divide and conquer"* part of *"the Establishment"* plan by recruiting and transporting thousands of Central Americans, and Muslims from the Middle East.

Veneer Republicans have now been shooting themselves in the foot as willing participants in *"the Establishment"* plan since the second Bush because they are enhancing the veneer Democrat's control of the U.S. Government.

Latinos, blacks and these others are not going to vote Republican in large numbers no matter how much they pander to "*leftist, liberal progressive*" minority "leaders" complicit in the plight of their constituencies growing beyond their ability to support their irresponsibly increasing numbers or contribute to the economic growth of the country.

The more illegal aliens granted amnesty, the faster Republicans are sealing the fate of their veneer of *"the Establishment," faux* "two party" system, and of the "America" that was once the destination for those desiring to better themselves through assimilation and contribution… rather than parasite on America's citizens and their dwindling resources.

The majority of these immigrants will vote for Democrats as long as it is the party that represents their values by offering the most Government largesse. This is the aspect of these cultures political correctness... also supported by some Republicans... has successfully inhibited Americans from discussing.

With some members of the Republican veneer of *"the Establishment"* being willing participants in the plans to destroy the "America" that once was by pandering to every special interest group except its conservative political base, the Second Bush Administration designated just *"another special interest group,"* and the *"leftist, liberal"* media lying and misrepresenting through the imposition of political correctness, what future is there for a united, prosperous America? Answer: very little.

Even though *"the house is burning down,"* don't count on the Republican Party veneer of *"the Establishment"* to act as the firemen for America.

It is entirely up to the American electorate to save America for themselves and their heirs. Americans, however, will not take the necessary action to accomplish this unless they become better educated about the *"the Establishment"* issues confronting them.

Therefore, they need to begin to understand the seriousness of *"the Establishment"* *"leftist, liberal progressive"* multicultural, politically correct, <u>*"New International Economic Order,"*</u> i.e., <u>*New World Order*</u>, One World Government threat to the future of a united, free and prosperous America. And they need to ensure they elect only leaders who represent their values, and have the testicular fortitude to act on their behalf in the best interests of all Americans, not in the interest of the Bush *"New World Order."*

So, for Mr. Keyes, Donald Trump, and all Americans, in an effort to prevent Russian Prime Minister Krushev's threat to then Vice President, Richard Nixon at Glassboro New Jersey in 1960, *"We will bury you* [America] *from within,"* becoming reality, the following pages are an effort to alert the American electorate to the facts, and reasons, their wonderful *"house"* that took over three hundred years to build is now, seriously, burning, and all who really care should not only be figuratively screaming, *"FIRE!"* but doing everything they can to extinguish it.

But how do they do this in addition to reading the following pages and learning the magnitude of the threat they are facing?

They could begin by making a "fire bucket brigade" start by rejecting another *"Establishment"* whore Bush, and electing a non-

"Establishment" member, non-politician, "fireman" businessman Republican Donald Trump as President of the U.S.

***

The author of this work who has a background in business turnarounds and management has been writing for years that the United States has been in serious need of a turnaround that no "professional" politician because of his chosen course in life would have the knowledge, ability or incentive to accomplish.

It would take a businessman with financial, organizational structure, high level interpersonal and management skills to understand the massive financial and other problems the country and its citizens have, and how to solve them.

Had the country ever had successful international businessmen in the position of Chief Executive Officer instead of political hacks motivated by obtaining money and power by implementing *"the Establishment"* America destroying policies for compensation or playing military leader without any military experience, the country would not have been, metaphorically; in the last minutes of the last quarter of the last game of the season with fourth down and ten facing it, and a "quarterback" with nothing but a string of losses behind him, which is where America was in 2016.

Fortunately, Trump possessing the experience and skills needed arrived ready to take over and save the "game," preventing another dubious, criminally dishonest, actually criminal effete *"elite Establishment"* whore with no experience other than being tenured in their club continue the destruction of America.

But even though he has all the delineated experience required to win and rebuild the country for success in the future, over half of the electorate prefers the criminal because they have *"no skin in the game"* of America, and if she were to win they would continue to be taken care of as they have been for decades without having to participate in America's capitalist economy by getting a job and taking care of themselves.

Thus, they do not desire Donald Trump, a patriot who spent $50 million of his own money to endeavor to save "America," and does not need additional money or power.

They selfishly prefer life-long communist Hillary Clinton whose loyalty is to *"the Establishment"* that *"bought and paid for"* her, and whose desire is continuance of the *NWO* destruction of

"America" for even more power and money.

So she, they and her anti-American *"Establishment"* co-conspirators will continue pursuance of America's destruction as a sovereign, independent, democratic nation even more vigorously given Trump is opposed to everything they want to do to America.

But, hopefully, the following will convince thinking members of the electorate to vote for Trump because those in the electorate, Government and media who prefer Hillary be President will continue aggressively pursuing Trump not win the Presidency because he is the only deterrence to their plans, as follow:

The Brzezinski Business Plan for America

Objective: to gain control of the U.S. Government and direct it toward the U.S. becoming a member of their envisioned *"New International Economic Order,"* i.e., *New World Order* with all countries under a One World Government like originally envisioned in creation of the United Nations, but with the realization that would require full support and cooperation from the top rungs of the U.S. economic ladder.

Therefore, to ensure these influential people would be on board with the concept of internationalizing or globalizing the world economy it must further enrich big business, the financial and political classes because their money and power were the basic requirements for success. But "unfortunately" the major source of the money had to be the pockets of taxpaying American citizens.

- *De facto* **Single Political Party:** control of the Government required controlling the Presidency, which meant controlling the two parties, or ideally having only one party. But given the U.S. system and human nature this would have to be *sub rosa,* i.e. under the surface, secret and confidential, not known to the U.S. electorate that must think they have a choice.

- *Sub Rosa* **Party Presidential Candidates:** of each veneer party must be a member of or committed to loyalty to the only single party actually in control. This would not be a problem because win or lose the election the candidates would be compensated via handsome financial compensation and/or positions for their loyalty and service by member or supporting business organizations or their veneer party organizations.

- **Enriching Business:** to obtain full support of big business they must be able to increase profits and value without waiting for slowly increasing gains from business as usual. They would need another means of accomplishing this widening of the spread between cost and revenue by producing at lower costs. Producing in lower cost countries like China and Mexico and being enabled to import those goods into the U.S. with no or minimal import duties would solve that problem.

- **Rewards:** corporate management would receive higher compensation, as would the financial class due to resultant increased profits and market capitalization, and the political class would also benefit because the growth of cash flowing to the business lobby would be increased tremendously enabling increased largesse available to it.

- **The Problem:** the American working, taxpaying Middle Class would lose jobs and suffer a wealth decline due to capital investment and production being moved offshore to enhance corporate profits, which would eventually, but sooner rather than later, cause unrest among these masses. Even though corporations could offer some products at lower prices, possibly slowing inflation, Middle Class historic economic gains and increasing wealth would be dramatically slowed, even reversed.

- **Solution Part I Control:** "Education" and Knowledge must be limited by imposing a loss of history to accomplish the required loss of knowledge of the American culture and economy that preceded the Brzezinski *"New World Order."*

Thus, as proven in Hitler Germany, Mao China even pre-reformation Catholic Europe that was the model for these two, it was necessary to control the minds of the people beginning with early education. Then controlling the media was an absolute must.

- **Solution Part II Change:** the nature of the population majority into one more accepting of more government control like those of Third World countries. In other, politically incorrect words a largely Government dependent, less well educated, less productive, complacent, passively governable population was needed. Solution: denizens of Mexico and other Third World Countries.

However, this would further adversely impact lives and finances of the principally Eurocentric majority population that would not be terribly receptive of the financial and lifestyle changes they would suffer, even after they were reduced to a minority, as planned.

- **Solution Part III More Control:** a <u>two-pronged solution;</u> take <u>control of their healthcare and disarm</u> the historically productive, controlling population, both slowly, but surely, as their electoral and physical power is reduced via mass immigration of the desired largely Government dependent third world immigrants.

The following chapters in this book present details on implementation of these Brzezinski/Rockefeller immoral plans *"the Establishment"* has ardently pursued since 1973 to secure control of the U.S. Government and accomplish their objectives of 1.) moving U.S. production offshore to increase corporate profits, 2.) changing education to indoctrination to control knowledge, 3.) creating a majority Government dependent electorate, 4.) implementing healthcare controls to control the people, and 5.) removing the ability of the people to defend themselves... all to enhance the wealth and power of *"the Establishment"* and their top one percent constituency to enable them to guide the country into their desired Brzezinski, *<u>"New International Economic Order</u>,"* i.e., *New World Order Socialist* One World Government, reducing American prosperity through trade deals and organizations to create *<u>"equilibrium"</u>* with other economies without consideration of cultural or other empirical differences with the ultimate goal of elimination of the *<u>"nation-state"</u>* all of which most Americans, if informed, would recognize is reality given the opposition to Trump and his *"Make [and keep] America Great Again"* plans.

STEP ONE: "*THE ESTABLISHMENT*"

CREATING AN ORGANIZATION DELIBERATELY INTENDED TO PLACE CONTROL OF AMERICA IN THE HANDS OF AN INSTITUTIONALIZED CORPORATE/GOVERNMENT PLUTOCRACY

The Webster Dictionary definition of "*the Establishment*" is… "*the plutocracy, regarded as holding the chief power and influence*" - "*the ruling inner circle of any nation, institution, etc.*" Further; "*plutocracy*" is defined as *"government by the wealthy" - "a group of wealthy people who control or influence a government."*

Therefore, by definition, America no longer has a Government "*of the people, by the people, for the people,*" which it probably, in reality, never did have.

But it did have, until just after the middle of the Twentieth Century, a Government that mostly functioned for the benefit of the majority of working, producing, taxpaying Americans, a Government of people who possessed the goals and objectives of the founders, who did their best to endeavor to make America the best place on earth for the people who lived and worked here.

But just after the middle of the century that changed. The government was taken over by… and since has been one hundred percent controlled for the benefit of… members of *"the Establishment"* who are destroying the "America" of yore, Ronald Reagan's "*shining city on a hill*" that was a beacon for freedom and prosperity. And they are willfully doing this for greed; greed for more money and power, which has more recently been even further facilitated.

"These men, largely private, were functioning on a level different from the public policy of the United States, and years later when New York times reporter Neil Sheehan read through the entire document [the history of the Vietnam war] *he would come away with one impression above all, which was that the Government of the United Sates was not what he had thought it was; it was as if there were an inner U.S. Government, what he called 'a centralized state, far more powerful than anything else, for whom the enemy is not simply the Communists but everything else, its*

own press, its own judiciary, its own Congress, foreign and friendly governments - all these are potentially antagonistic. It had survived and perpetuated itself, often using the issue of anti-Communism as a weapon against the other branches of government and the press, and finally, it does not function necessarily for the benefit of the Republic but rather for its own ends, its own perpetuation: it has its own codes which are quite different from public codes. Secrecy was a way of protecting itself, not so much from threats from foreign governments, but from detection from its own population on charges of its own competence and wisdom.' Each succeeding Administration was careful, once in office not to expose the weaknesses of its predecessor. After all, essentially the same people were running the governments, they had continuity to each other... Thus, the national security apparatus kept its continuity, and every outgoing President tended to rally to the side of each incumbent President."   - David Halberstam, THE BEST AND THE BRIGHTEST, 1973

This ironically published the year Brzezinski and Rockefeller formalized "*the Establishment*" organization confirms there has long been a cabal of continuity... "*Shadow Government, Deep State*" or whatever one chooses to call it... in charge of the U.S. Government regardless who the people elect to represent them.

This was further proven in 2010 when Obama was President. The U.S. Supreme Court again ruled against the people in favor of "*the Establishment*" in its *Citizens United* ruling that proved it is as politicized as the FBI Director proved he is in his decision not to recommend charges on Hillary's Email criminal actions.

In this decision it essentially ensured "*the Establishment*" will become more firmly entrenched in its control of the U.S. Government by eliminating limits on campaign spending by corporations and labor unions, and limiting the possibility of preventing corruption in campaign financing, potentially creating a system of unlimited bribery.

Now big money from these entities and the very rich will substantially offset votes of average Americans and thwart the democratic process because big money will satisfy the extant greed of lobbyists, politicians, heads of Government agencies, and the rest of "*the Establishment.*"

It should be noted this decision was also rendered under supposedly conservative Chief Justice John Roberts, appointed by second generation *bona fide* "Establishment" actor, to be kind, George W. Bush, the same Court that also ruled in favor of the "*Individual Mandate*" in Obamacare, unconstitutionally permitting the Government to force citizens to pay a corporation for something they might not desire by ruling it a criminal act not to do so, which seems a strange form of "*Justice.*"

But Americans have no reason to expect "*justice*" from their Government. Given its anti-Trump actions by top FBI and "Justice" Officials in 2016 as well commentary by other "Security" Department heads and other information, indicating likely involvement in anti-Trump activities by so many others they should be afraid of "their" Government, as they should have been for over forty years prior.

The Day America [that was] Died

"America" was changed after November 22, 1963, the day President John F. Kennedy was assassinated.

Had he remained alive, as President, JFK would likely have stopped the invasion of Vietnam and the following twelve years of useless war costing fifty-eight thousand American lives, tens of thousands of seriously wounded and hundreds of thousands of Vietnamese lives, as well as the death of the "America" that was… the "America" of promise and prosperity that has also since been further brutalized by more unnecessary war and unbridled expansion of the Government permitted by inflation of the monetary base through Federal Reserve issued *fiat* currency not backed by silver or anything else.

That day Kennedy died was the day the real "America" died. That day was the zenith of the American dream, and the death of it and the concept of the "America" that existed since 1776.

But it was also the day those willfully destroying that "America" for decades for personal gain began to seize a firm grip on the tiller of the United States ship of state prevailed over the dream, the concept and the people of "America."

Shortly after taking office after Kennedy's death, President

Johnson reversed JFK's June 1963 Executive Order 11110 that authorized the Government treasury to again begin issuing silver certificates, U.S. currency backed by the nation's silver reserves, essentially curtailing Federal Reserve control of the money supply and limiting it to the availability of silver in the reserves or what the economy could afford based on Government tax revenues.

This potentially limited expansion of the Government and its activities like unnecessary wars and the planned societal destruction of Johnson's "*Great Society*" that implemented "welfare," food stamps, subsidized housing and other programs eliminating the need to work, and was also the first step toward the *"divide and conquer"* part of *"the Establishment"* plan in that it encouraged the breakup of the black family by rewarding black female mothers financially for not being married.

Then after rescinding the Executive Order Johnson began removing Silver Certificates from circulation, and the Federal Reserve began, in earnest, the issuance of *fiat* currency… money out of thin air that carries an interest cost payable to it by the Government, but is not redeemable for gold or silver from Government reserves, i.e., free money that permits unaffordable Government expansion without cost except to the American people thru interest payments to the TBTF banks, denigration of their purchasing power, and impoverishment through inflation.

Johnson also expedited the buildup for the Vietnam invasion, then he and others in the Government created the Gulf of Tonkin false flag event, lied to the American people and United Nations, and officially began that conflict in earnest.

By the time he left office in January 1969, following in FDR's footsteps, he was responsible for tremendous unnecessary war costs in lives and money, massive Government expansion through his *"Great Society"* welfare programs and spending more than all previous Presidents combined, beginning a seemingly unstoppable spending spree of continuing destruction.

***

July 1973… just shy of ten years after President Kennedy's death… the most widely unknown important event having the most adverse long term effect on Americans, their economic well-being, security, freedoms, and future occurred.

David Rockefeller, then Chairman of Chase Manhattan Bank, the youngest of the six children of oil baron and world's richest man John D. Rockefeller's son, John D. Rockefeller Jr., and Harvard PhD Zbigniew Brzezinski founded the formal organization that has become the preeminent organization of the America destroying *"Establishment."*

To understand the nature and character of this organization and the effect its members are having on Americans and their country consider the following:

- Rockefeller stated in response to a characterization of him as internationalist, conspiring with others around the world to build a more integrated global political and economic structure—one world, if you will, ***"If that's the charge, I stand guilty, and I am proud of it."***

- He is also credited with the statement ***"Americans have too much democracy."***

- Polish born Democrat Zbigniew Brzezinski attended Harvard to work on a doctorate he received in 1953, later collaborated on study of concept of totalitarianism, and supported Johnson's Presidential campaign and *"Great Society."*

- He also supported the Vietnam War and selected Jimmy Carter he claimed to have groomed for three years to be President as a member of the organization before Carter announced his candidacy for President in 1976.

- Carter proclaimed himself an *"eager student"* of Brzezinski who became his foreign policy advisor, and appointed him his National Security Advisor.

- In 1979 Brzezinski led the United States in a new arms buildup. In an interview he admitted the U.S. supported radical Islamists to undermine Russia.

- He also admitted U.S. covert action got Russia to start the Afghan war in 1979.

- Asked if he had regrets about this, he responded, ***"Regret what? That secret operation was an excellent idea. It had the effect of drawing the Russians into the Afghan trap and you want me to regret it? The day that the Soviets officially crossed the border, I wrote to President Carter: We now have the opportunity of giving to the USSR its Vietnam War."***

24

- When asked if he regrets having given arms and advice to future terrorists he responded, *"What is most important to the history of the world? The Taliban or the collapse of the Soviet empire? Some stirred-up Muslims or the liberation of Central Europe and the end of the Cold War?"*

- When he was told, *"Islamic fundamentalism represents a world menace today."* Brzezinski responded, *"Nonsense! It is said that the West had a global policy in regard to Islam. That is stupid. There isn't a global Islam…."* [Le Nouvel Observateur (Paris), 1/15/1998]

- In 2008 Democratic Presidential candidate Obama obtained the endorsement of and foreign policy advice of Brzezinski who chose and groomed him as he did Carter, and once endorsed the creation and support of militant Islamic forces in Afghanistan that were directed by accused "9/11" mastermind Osama bin Laden.

- Obama has since stated, *"I've learned an immense amount from Dr. Brzezinski who is one of our country's most outstanding scholars who has done a lot for our country."*

- In 2016 Hillary Clinton went on the campaign trail with Obama signifying she agrees with, and would represent continuation of "*the* [Brzezinski] *Establishment*" policy of wars for purposes other than protection of America, as well as the position "*There isn't a global Islam*" Obama followed like a good little puppet of Brzezinski who claimed to have created and groomed him for the Presidency for four years, regardless of the continuing death toll of Americans and many others throughout the world.

***

In light of the above is there any doubt <u>Hillary</u> who also <u>refuses to acknowledge Islamic terrorism,</u> was a member and sometime <u>chair of the "*leftist*" New World Foundation</u> from 1982 to 1988, would be anything other than just a continuation, like so many other members of "*the Establishment,*" Democrat and Republican alike, who have been responsible for most of the bad policies, actions and destruction Americans have suffered since 1973?

Examples of what members of this unsavory "*Establishment*" have wrought are elimination of conscription to create a military non-representative of the population so it will not protest unnecessary wars as it did the Vietnam War, the foundation for moving U.S. capital investment, production and jobs offshore to enhance corporate profits for the benefit of their executives and the political *"Establishment,"* forcing management, i.e., control, of trillions of dollars of retirement money into a few hands on Wall Street, enhancing banks, corporations and politicians at the expense of retirees, the massive U.S. arms buildup, more wars like the 2014 U.S. *coup d' état* in the Ukraine and starting a new Cold War with Russia, both of which are, per advice from Brzezinski in his 1997 book, necessary to remove Russia as an obstacle to their desired *New World Order* One World Government, and ensuring Americans are unaware of this by keeping it a secret through control of the media.

***

But as bad as all of this is, consider the following some attribute to Saul Alinsky who wrote <u>Rules for Radicals</u> that was inspirational for *"Counter-Culture"* college organizers, as well as Caesar Chavez, Jesse Jackson, Hillary Clinton and Barrack Obama.

Although some say he wrote them and others say he didn't, these exact statements cannot be found in this book. But he wrote a lot, they are not far off his admitted communist leanings, and someone wrote them, also in sympathy with communist philosophy... even possibly Hillary, since she was close to him, and they describe what appears to be her agenda for America.

These instructions on how to create a socialist state, no matter who wrote them, represent an outline of what has been done in America over the past forty years:

1) Healthcare. Control healthcare and control the people.

2) Poverty. Increase the Poverty level as high as possible. Poor people are easier to control and will not fight back if they are provided everything for them to live.

3) Debt. Increase the debt to an unsustainable level. That way you are able to increase taxes, and this will produce more poverty.

4) Gun Control. Remove the ability to defend themselves from the Government. That way you are able to create a police state.

5) Welfare. Take control of every aspect of their lives (Food, Housing, and Income).

6) Education. Take control of what people read and listen to, and what children learn in school.

7) Religion. Remove the belief in the God from the Government and schools.

8) Class Warfare - Divide people into the wealthy and poor. This will cause more discontent and it will be easier to take (Tax) the wealthy with the support of the poor.

These points represent a simplification of much of the <u>Communist Manifesto</u> used by Russian communists to convert and subdue the Russian people Stalin described as *"Useful Idiots."*

Alinsky born of Jewish Russian immigrants died in 1972, the year before the official creation of the organization whose members were in control of America for forty years as of 2016, *"the Establishment."*

But for the benefit of those who might doubt this is happening in the U.S., or Alinsky influenced those in control… and one who could potentially be in control… of America, let's look at the influence of his teachings.

<u>But first,</u> note: Hillary did her college thesis on Alinsky's writings with his personal assistance, and when Bill became President this thesis was removed from public access. Why, we can only guess since Hillary has been described as a *"leftist"* legal scholar whose first law internship was with an Oakland, CA law firm that supported "radical causes," including the Black Panthers, and whose two partners were communists.

Obama also writes about him in his books, likely in addition to sympathy with his *"Counter* [American] *Culture"* ideas, because he was also the founder of "community organizing," which he began in Chicago where Obama engaged in the same under his guidelines that also influenced his 2008 Presidential campaign.

Many argue about *"conspiracy theory"…* mostly those in, or in support of *"the Establishment"…* to endeavor to disavow or disprove what those with minds unobstructed by indoctrination or an inability to connect the dots can easily "see." For there to be a *"conspiracy"* only two people have to conspire, i.e., combine for evil purposes, plot, or devise.

There is no evidence Hillary and Obama conspired to do what was in both their minds fifteen years apart. But implementing the same program near the beginning of their tenures in the White House should cause recognition of the high priority both gave this action for which the idea to do the same thing at the same relative time came from a common source or sources.

Given the two people Hillary and Obama had a connection with or for whose ideas stated admiration are Brzezinski and Alinsky, and both were influenced by these two in their actions to hasten creation of a *"socialist state"* in America fifteen years apart, indicates a high degree of probability of, at least, collusion.

1) Healthcare. Go back to shortly after the Clintons were in the White House. Hillary secretly developed a "healthcare" plan "to control the people" via cards that had to be presented to receive healthcare. These cards were geographically limited. Also there was much more in the plan that caused it to be rejected at that time.

Now, flip forward a decade and a half after further dumbing down of and lying to the people as well as Congress, the installation of an *"Establishment"* Supreme Court Chief Justice who was willing to ignore the Constitution and bend the law, and *violá;* The Affordable Care Act... that was not "affordable."

Surely anyone who was an adult in 1993 could recognize the similarity of the two plans and connect the dots between these two and their mutual mentors.

2) Poverty. Since 2008; fewer jobs, millions more unemployed, lower pay and household income, more citizens on food stamps, interest rates so low people could not get any income on their savings, need we say more?

3) Debt. Obama almost doubled this, increasing it to an amount in excess of the *faux* national Gross Domestic Product, by increasing Government debt an amount unequaled by all Presidents during the 220 plus years prior to him.

4) Gun Control. Democrats, especially Hillary and Obama have consistently campaigned against citizens owning guns, i.e., against the Second Amendment.

5) Welfare. This has been greatly expanded under all Democrats since Lyndon Johnson's *"Great Society"* in 1965 that also satisfied numbers 2) and 3) by tremendously increasing debt by an amount, as Obama has, greater than all previous Presidents.

6) Education. This has been deliberately, greatly denigrated in the decades since Jimmy Carter formed the Department of Education. It has been changed from educating to indoctrinating by

"teaching" what to think and eliminating history, the language and geography so the people will lose their culture, and not be able to recognize what the Government is doing to them. Check out the "common core" of public education.

7) Religion. Everyone is aware it has been under attack by Democrats for years.

8) Class Warfare. This has been a major program of *"the Establishment"* through its *"divide and conquer"* program for over fifty years as of 2016.

All this destruction is the result of actions by many like Hillary and Obama being greatly influenced by the ideas of *"the Establishment"* represented by Brzezinski and others like Alinsky advocating implementation of *"leftist"* programs destructive to "America" and its people.

Now, three questions: a) does anyone doubt the "America" they have known and loved has been deliberately destroyed by members of *"the Establishment"* like Lyndon Johnson, Jimmy Carter, Hillary Clinton, Barrack Obama, Brzezinski, Rockefeller and scores of other, mostly Democrat, members of *"the Establishment,"* b) how was this destruction accomplished, and c) how could anyone other than one of Stalin's *"Useful Idiots"* vote to install anyone else as President who is desirous of continuing and even expanding this destruction of converting a freedom providing and prosperous "America" to what will eventually become a totalitarian *"Socialist"* police state?

The answer to a) is hopefully *"no"* because *"yes"* equals *"Useful Idiot,"* and it would mean America is definitely done for. c) provides its own answer. So let's look at b).

A booklet entitled <u>Members of the Club</u> published several years before this writing disclosed many companies and individuals who were at one time members of *"the Establishment"* organization created by Rockefeller and Brzezinski in 1973. Here is a partial list of companies it says either have, or had, senior members of management represented among the membership:

General Electric Corporation (which owns NBC, CNBC and MSNBC), *US NEWS AND WORLD REPORT,* CNN, *WASHINGTON POST, NEW YORK TIMES,* Time Warner Corporation, Xerox, Archer Daniels Midland, PepsiCo, Molson

Companies, Goldman Sachs, RJR Nabisco, TRW, American International (AIG), Levi Strauss Company, Corning, S.C. Johnson, Coca Cola, Exxon Mobil, General Motors, Smith Kline Beecham, Nissan, NEC, Sony Corporation, Toshiba, IBM, Toyota, Ford, Chase Manhattan Bank and Citibank.

Additionally, here are some individuals it states have been members you might recognize:

George H.W. Bush, Alan Greenspan, Lawrence Eagleburger, Walter Mondale, Tom Ridge, Bill Clinton, Charles Rangel, John Danforth, John Chafee, Strob Talbot, Casper Weinberger, Alan Simpson, Diane Feinstein, Donna Shalala, William Cohen, Charles Robb, George Schultz, Brent Scowcroft, Andrew Young, Paul Volker.

Given this list includes large media, pharmaceutical, auto, personal products, energy, technology, banks and other companies, as well as Presidents, their senior staff and cabinet members, senators, chairman of the Federal Reserve and other highly influential people, question b) "how was this destruction accomplished" should be answered. But that is not the end of it.

Early fall 2016 Wolf Blitzer on CNN cited some of these names who are Republicans saying they would be voting for Hillary Clinton in an effort to discredit Trump's Presidential bid without pointing out, as he obviously knew, they were doing this because they are members of the same club as the Clintons, Bushes and others whose *New World Order* continuing destruction of America for personal gain could be stopped by Trump.

The next day, September 20, 2016, it was announced Trump was neck and neck with Hillary for electoral votes. Also, while showing a photo of the enfeebled ex-President, long term member of *"the Establishment"* Trilateral club, C.I.A. and many more America destroying activities it was announced George H. W. Bush would be voting for Hillary.

The fact of all the prominent Republicans voting for Hillary rather than Trump was an effort to further lessen Trump's chances because all these characters were aware they and their controlled media had been successful in depriving Americans of knowledge of the Trilateral Commission they were all members of and beholding to, rather than their Democrat and Republican veneer of their one big party affiliations.

***

For almost half a century U.S. Government policies have been guided by *"the Establishment"* because of the highly placed officials, including all U.S. Presidents since Carter, except Ronald Reagan, who have either been, or appointed by members.

<u>The U.S. job destroying, "free trade" treaties like NAFTA, the American culture destroying immigration policies, billions of dollars to Mexico and Africa, and appeasement of Arab regimes regarding the Arab/Israeli conflict are all a result of *"the Establishment," New World Order* influences within the U.S. Government.</u>

Like most of these actions and agreements, the Trans Pacific Partnership has been promoted by Obama to continue the damage to America, its people and economy.

It is like the other U.S. "trade" agreements *"the Establishment"* entered into to the detriment of America...just another *New World Order* "globalization" trade deal that, like the WTO, World Trade Organization, agreements and NAFTA, is designed to disadvantage Americans by setting rules to further enhance the coffers of multinational corporations, "trampling democracy, national sovereignty and the public good."

As Donald Trump accurately states, *"It is a rigged system!"* that has adversely affected Americans as Ross Perot pointed out over two decades ago: *"In the 1960s, our standard of living doubled every generation and a half. At our present low growth rate, it will take twelve generations for our standard of living to double."*

Almost everything has gotten worse since the *1960s*.

In the intervening years since JFK's death the United States has been at war unnecessarily, on a preemptive basis for over twenty-five years, almost fifty percent of the time, in countries that posed no threat to the security of the United States.

The U.S. military has been greatly expanded into occupations in more than one hundred and twenty countries. The "defense" industry has experienced phenomenal growth, as has the wealth of those involved in it.

The Government has greatly expanded control over the people, and Bush II began deemphasizing the title of Chief Executive Officer of the United States, a position that desperately needed to be competently filled, favoring Commander-in-Chief of the United States Military, clearly demonstrating the misplaced priorities of "*the Establishment*" Barrack Obama studiously followed... nay, greatly expanded, as Hillary will should she become President of the United States.

One of those priorities is taking as much money as possible from every productive citizen to continue to fund the out of control Government failed financial basket case, generating only half the revenues it needed from the economy caused by *"the Establishment"* membership incompetence of Bush II and Obama.

"America" likely could not withstand another four or eight years of an *"Establishment"* President. That would likely be the absolute end of "America" as we know it.

No matter what anyone thinks about Donald Trump, <u>he is the only non-"*Establishment*" choice</u>, even if he were not the competent international businessman at the right time in America's history he is.

He does NOT represent *"the Establishment"* represented by Hillary and Obama, and Republicans like Jeb Bush, John McCain, Mitt Romney, and others who refused to support him, and even campaigned against him, like William Kristol who "showed his stripes" by endeavoring to get a third party candidate to run against Trump for the purpose of ensuring Hillary would be elected.

All these *"Establishment"* whores have demonstrated where their loyalty lies through these actions: they and the rest of their Republican ilk would much prefer the *status quo* destruction course for "America" represented by Hillary because they have been beneficiaries of it.

STEP TWO: TRADE

DELIBERATELY INCREASING CORPORATE PROFITS AT THE   EXPENSE OF AMERICA'S MIDDLE CLASS AND ECONOMY

When Brzezinski and Rockefeller founded their organization in July 1973 that would soon thereafter become the breeding ground for the population of "*the Establishment*" we have had for four decades they knew what they were doing. They had **The Business Plan for America** presented above at the end of the Prologue.

Rockefeller was fifty-eight, attended Harvard and the London School of Economics with John Kennedy, was already the head of one of the biggest banks in the world, Chase Manhattan bank, in 2016 J.P. Morgan Chase, that did business with other big banks worldwide, big oil and others, and was heavily involved in international trade, which enabled him to count among his friends leaders of big businesses around the world.

He was also an "insider" with the CIA, and already expressed his support for a *"one world,"* in a way that connotes one world government or political establishment, or what could be interpreted as his not placing the good or wellbeing of the U.S. foremost. Incidentally, he also visited China in 1973.

Brzezinski was forty-five, a descendent of Polish nobility from part of that country that is now the Ukraine. He also attended Harvard where, as stated before, he received his Doctorate.

He spent his pre-pubescent youth in Hitler Germany, Russia and Canada where he grew up before coming to the U.S. He was an advisor to both Presidents Kennedy and Johnson before his positions with Carter.

Rockefeller classified himself a Republican, although seemingly a very moderate one. Brzezinski was a Democrat. No question. These credentials and experiences provided both with sufficient credibility to claim their new organization was "bipartisan," which it definitely was and continues to be, as demonstrated by the bilateral... some might say *"speaking from both sides of its mouth"*... makeup of the one party, *faux* "two party" system sham we have in American politics.

Their Business Plan took into account the necessity of appeal to both veneers of the *faux "two party"* system because it was necessary for them to appeal to both veneers *of "the Establishment"* to accumulate the money and power they desired and needed for their plan to be successful. They knew money was the key to the power their plan was all about…as it always is.

After formalizing *"the Establishment"* organization, STEP TWO that was actually a broad based "trade" plan… both had to know was bad for Americans and their economy… was begun to get as much more money as possible into corporate coffers. And they knew where the money was, and how to generate it.

***

<u>In 1973, before these two, the U.S. was still the largest, richest and most powerful business and industrial economy in the world.</u> It was still a net exporter of oil. Also, China's internal conflict that began with Mao's Communist Revolution in the early 1920s ended with Mao's success in 1947, a quarter century prior to 1973.

In the next quarter century ended, conveniently, just before Rockefeller and Brzezinski's "business" venture began, China had begun to put its billion people population back to work, and was producing and exporting on a massive, wealth creating scale consistent with the country's prior history of almost two millennia.

This was the key to their plan. And as is oft said, *"Timing is everything."*

The decades long prohibition on trading with communist China, a defined enemy of *"the Establishment"* at the time, was lifted by the U.S. in April 1971, two years prior, but the U.S. ostensibly still did not have diplomatic relations with the country, which was a limitation on what big business corporations were willing to do there.

The British colony of Hong Kong was different. It was a longtime bustling hub of business activity, much of it with the U.S.

On its Victoria Island there was much wealth on display. In the Kowloon part of the colony that was on the Chinese mainland there were massive port facilities.

What was the real source of all this activity and wealth?

Short answer: China. Long answer: a combination of British organization, unfettered capitalism, the long ostensible aversion of U.S. *"Establishment"* hypocrites to anything communist, and

China. But without China the other three would have been meaningless.

To demonstrate this there were many examples of suppliers of such items as furniture, housewares, electronics and other items widely used in the U.S. located on the island in high rise, predominately office buildings in a highly congested, densely populated area where space was very expensive.

There were also many in Kowloon where one would expect to find manufacturing facilities, but some of them desired to be in the commercial area on the island, rather than the industrial area, and they could afford it

These usually had a small office and one other room in one of the multistory office buildings. The office was not huge or fancy. It was just adequate and comfortable for conducting the business of selling to one or two people at a time. In the other room would usually be no more than four Chinese working, producing one or two of the items the supplier was selling.

How could businesses like his with such small production afford the space?

Answer: the fact was; hardly anything was made or manufactured in Hong Kong except the red and blue Union Jack *"Made in Hong Kong"* labels and tags these workers, like thousands of others were usually engaged in placing on all the merchandise actually made in China headed for the U.S. as they unloaded it from trucks that brought it from mainland, communist China before putting it into shipping containers in Kowloon that were headed to the United States.

Hong Kong's business was never manufacturing. It has always been a financial and distribution center. Its wealth and manmade physical awesomeness were entirely attributable to it being the major distribution point for products manufactured by a billion plus Chinese communists.

Everything in stores, and everywhere else in the U.S. sporting *"Made in Hong Kong,"* red, white and blue British Union Jack labels, tags and U.S required "*Made In*" stickers, labels and printing on packages was made in mainland China by Chinese communist workers.

This was well known by most of the hypocrites in the U.S. Government *"Establishment,"* especially David Rockefeller who visited China, and probably Hong Kong in 1973… if he was required to go through there to get to the mainland as ordinary Americans and business people were required to.

They were aware of the enormous labeling operation named "Hong Kong," and that they had no ability to do anything about it through U.S. businesses because they were buying from vendors in Hong Kong representing their merchandise was made there.

But stopping this was not what the U.S. Government, *"the Establishment"* corporations, financial institutions or Rockefeller and Brzezinski were interested in doing.

They were assiduously pursuing legitimizing, maximizing and participating in the enormous profit potential of Chinese manufacturing for years before this time, but they recently turned on the afterburners in this effort, and were in the process of accomplishing it.

In April of 1971, two years prior, the U.S. ended its blockade of China and its ban on China trade after U.S. National Security Advisor, Henry Kissinger, paid the Chinese a visit. Then in October of that year Taiwan was expelled from the United Nations and replaced by China. After the U.S. ping pong team was there in November, China was given a seat on the U.N. Security Council.

The planning to pave the way for U.S. production to be moved to China to fatten profits of U.S. corporations and enhance their market capitalizations, thus lining the pockets of their executives and filling the coffers of U.S. politicians… unnecessarily, at the expense of American workers, the manufacturing based American Middle Class, productive capability, and ultimately economy and wealth of the "America" that was… was *fait accompli.*

The only task for Rockefeller and Brzezinski was to get U.S. Corporations to start the ball rolling in a big way to begin manufacturing in China where they were not burdened with U.S. Governmental regulations, unions, costs of facility construction and, of course, U.S. high wages so they would have enhanced cash flow and market capitalizations. But this did not take long.

The U.S. Liaison Office was opened in Peking in 1973. Then, in August 1974 one of the members of the Brzezinski/Rockefeller organization from the beginning, and longtime C.I.A. member George H.W. Bush, was appointed Chief of the Office. The rest is, as is said, *"History."* And that *"History"* ain't pretty for working, taxpaying Middle Class Americans!

Since that time U.S. wages have stagnated, productive capacity utilization declined, as has the investment in plant and equipment, etc., etc. to the extent some estimate fifty percent of the dollar value of shipments from China to the U.S. are attributable to American companies producing their products in China and importing them to the U.S. practically duty and tariff free.

What Ross Perot stated in 1992 was a rosy scenario. The U.S. standard of living has continued to decline since 1974.

Corporate coffers have bulged as Rockefeller and Brzezinski planned, corporate executive compensation wherein CEOs were making eight or ten times their employees in the 1970s, are now paid hundreds of times the salaries of their employees, Government salaries are fifty to one hundred percent higher than those of employees in the real, productive economy, Congressional salaries are more than three times what they were in 1980, and... at the expense of American workers... many American corporations are producing more and making more money from their interests in China than in the U.S. Example: in 2016 General Motors produced more autos in China than in the U.S.

Meanwhile, the Chinese are getting richer because they do not have their money taken from them by their government to enable it to engage in foreign interventions, and other *New World Order,* unnecessary actions.

So, the Rockefeller/**<u>Brzezinski Business Plan for America</u>** was wildly successful for them. They got the money flowing where they desired, and Americans have less democracy.

***

This legacy should be sufficient to cause conscientious, thinking Americans to strongly desire not to have members of *"the Establishment"* that wrought all this destruction remain in charge of the U.S. Government, but there is more, especially from the Democrat veneer of the *faux* "two party" system. Some of it even before the Rockefeller/Brzezinski organization was formalized.

Post WWII the Democrat controlled Congress was directly responsible for destroying the U.S. steel industry by refusing to permit sufficient depreciation and amortization to provide cash flow needed to upgrade and replace its turn of the century, 1900s fossil fuel powered blast furnaces and other productive facilities to maintain competitiveness with Japan's new electric furnaces.

Meanwhile it was the same Democrats who were responsible for the new emerging, dominant Japanese steel industry.

Even during the Democrat, Vietnam War in the 1960s when the U.S. had a *"Buy America"* policy, the U.S. Government was buying Japanese steel to satisfy its war requirements. (In 2016, that would still be a problem, except they would be able to supplement Japanese steel with purchases from South Korea and China.)

But speaking of the Vietnam War; during that fiasco by the Johnson administration some U.S. "defense" production was moved to South Korea. That "some" was sufficient to provide a kick to the South Korean economy that resulted in it growing by five hundred percent in just a few years.

The $250 million the Johnson administration paid the South Korean Government to provide troops for the Vietnam endeavor could have also assisted.

One more example: during the 1960s and into the seventies *"the Establishment"* was also successful in destroying two more American industries.

They literally drove U.S. ocean surface shipping out of business by imposing Government determined freight charges on all U.S. flag carriers carrying shipments to all U.S. ports, and they imposed/dictated employee union wages on U.S. flag vessels that were greatly in excess of those paid on foreign flag vessels.

As a result of these rules the U.S. companies were prohibited from successfully competing in the worldwide market by those who style themselves as champions of *"free trade."*

Thus, many years prior to 2016, U.S. shipping companies were gone along with thousands of jobs and billions of dollars of contribution to the U.S. economy.

Along with the U.S. shipping industry went the U.S commercial shipbuilding industry, and who knows how many jobs, as well as more billions of dollars of contribution to the economy.

South Korea has further benefited from these U.S. Government actions by becoming one of the few major producers of large oceangoing freight and commodity transport vessels.

For at least three decades, thanks to members of *"the Establishment,"* all the manufactured goods shipped to the U.S. from China, Japan, Korea, and elsewhere are shipped on vessels likely made in Korea of Korean, Chinese or Japanese steel, flying flags other than American and owned by foreign based companies.

Don't believe this? Go to any major American port and look at the names and flags on the ships and the containers they are carrying. Then try to envisage how many hundreds and hundreds of thousands of lost American jobs and trillions of dollars of contribution to the U.S, economy all this represents.

It is impossible to begin to imagine how Americans could do this to their country and their countrymen. But facts are; they have.

<u>The important, obvious fact is: clearly, *"the Establishment"* are not friends of Americans. They must be... as shown by their actions... *"One world"* internationalists of the ilk of David Rockefeller who, like he and Brzezinski, are willing to sacrifice the prosperity, lives and future of America on President Bush's stated *New World Order* altar of personal greed solely for M-O-N-E-Y.</u>

***

Here are some other egregious examples:

First, as previously addressed, Bill Clinton who oversaw the NAFTA moving to Mexico of manufacturing vehicles, appliances and much more that were doing just fine in the U.S., providing profits for American corporations and continuing to enrich and enlarge a large part of the still growing, at the time of his "election," great American Middle Class.

Why would he do that... being the smart guy he is... when he knew it would adversely affect the entire U.S. economy, driving a big stake into the heart of the economic well-being of the manufacturing based American Middle Class, driver of a large part of the economy he was supposed to represent, as Ross Perot told everyone, including Bill, during the election campaign this is what would happen?

Well, we can only guess. But again indications are it was M-O-N-E-Y, pure and simple, because when he entered the White

House financial disclosures indicated he had a net worth of $250,000 to $400.000 even after Hillary's controversial conversion of $1,000 into $100,000 in ten months "trading" cattle futures.

In 2016 Bill and Hillary are reportedly worth $50 to $100 million, likely much more if the strange Clinton Global Initiative that has received many tens of millions of dollars of contributions from many foreign regimes... for what unknown purpose... is included.

This by a couple holding no wealth producing positions other than engagements speaking to the heads of those contributing foreign regimes and members of the U.S. plutocracy for which they were paid hundreds of thousands for each speech.

Next, probably to the dismay of diehard, but self-imposed ignorant Republicans: George W. Bush who would not have been President if not for his father who has a decades long history of serving no one but "*the Establishment*" in each of the offices he was given for that purpose.

It is not possible for anyone not to know the damage he did to America as President with the absolutely unnecessary, strategic blunder, Iraq fiasco that has cost trillions of dollars to date, and was a major transfer of wealth to "defense" industry members of "*the Establishment.*"

This also qualifies as one of the bad trade deals for Americans because the bulk of these funds were spent outside the U.S., rewarding others.

Also, No one could be so intellectually lacking as to not understand what he did, and why he did it for the benefit of "*the Establishment*" member, agricultural company, Archer Daniels Midland unless they are ignorant of this action.

So let's also ask why he is responsible for legislating converting corn, a worldwide basic food source, to energy, driving up its price, and adversely affecting hundreds of millions, when Brazilian sugar cane ethanol was at least fifty cents a gallon less expensive and would not have adversely affected anyone?

Further, let's ask why he oversaw creation of a new pharmaceutical Part D Medicare in which he specifically excluded pharmaceutical prices being negotiated on behalf of millions of elderly Americans paying for them, thus enhancing pharmaceutical companies' ability to greatly increase profits by taking more money from the pockets of these older Americans in need of those drugs whose interests he was supposed to be representing, as well as also further, greatly enhancing profits of insurance companies?

Should anyone doubt he did this they should look at the billions of dollars pharmaceutical companies spend on TV advertising for prescription drugs, including those made by foreign companies, and the multi-million dollar a year position and benefits package the Louisiana congressman who pushed this through Congress for Bush received in his new position as head of the pharmaceutical Congressional lobbying group he resigned from Congress to take immediately after passage of this legislation.

Also, some might wonder if they were aware of it: why did the head of the Harvard University Endowment, a friend of George H.W. Bush, authorize in the late 1980s the largest ever, before that time, single investment by the endowment in the failing oil company in which George W. Bush was a board member?

Possibly because shortly thereafter, before he became Governor of Texas, he received millions of dollars for his stock.

M-O-N-E-Y! *"The Establishment"* America destroying greed and corruption will go on and on until there is nothing left unless it is stopped by a non-*"Establishment"* President Trump.

For as an esteemed Harvard Business School professor stated to his class in 1969:

> ***"The economy that does not produce the things it consumes or uses will not survive."***

STEP THREE: EDUCATION

TAKING CONTROL OF WHAT PEOPLE READ AND LISTEN TO AND WHAT CHILDREN LEARN IN SCHOOL

Before 1973, thinking was not a threat to the government. It was still encouraged in education system classrooms. But 1973 was the year the evil creeping toward control of America since the time of Kennedy's assassination was formalized, and unfortunately for "America," knew "education" was the key to the success of their desired *"placidly governable,"* indoctrinated population.

The founder of that "evil," along with David Rockefeller of *"too much democracy,"* Zbigniew Brzezinski, wrote in his 1970 book about the desirability of... ***"the gradual appearance of a more controlled society... dominated by an elite unrestrained by traditional values"*** **that could exploit** ***"the latest techniques to manipulate emotions and control reason"*** **of individuals who are** ***"citizens"*** of America... and presumably everywhere else.

It is impossible to differentiate this idea from those of communist leaders rightly vilified by numerous American "leaders" and the U.S. media for decades.

Brzezinski is the architect of the Orwellian Totalitarian state desired by *"the Establishment"* developing since the beginning of the Twenty First Century in America. He was a willful unmitigated proactive proponent of the destruction of personal freedom, individualism and free will of humans who are to be completely subjugated to the will of despots who control everything in America and the rest of the world... and willing to reward him for his assistance in the destruction of all advances of mankind since the Magna Carta in the year 1215.

It was not an accident this "man" was chosen National Security Advisor to President Carter, the "evil's" first puppet President and ostensible creator of the... surprise!... Department of "Education," elected entirely through the understanding of the importance of religion in all cultures, including the Christian culture in the United States.

After using religion on the unsuspecting electorate to get into office, Carter acted quickly under the direction of his puppet master, Brzezinski who was responsible for his being President, to

42

eliminate what they perceived the biggest threat to their ability to take and keep control of the country's economic and military power.

The planned "educational" destruction of knowledge, free thought and the ability to reason, as promulgated by Brzezinski, through his advocated *"controlled society"* was immediately instigated, presumably under the direction of this "man" as "National Security Advisor," thereby also providing to us the knowledge of what *"the Establishment"* members in the U.S. Government and media really mean when they refer to *"national security."* It is their security they refer to, not that of the nation or people of America.

The act of Carter putting "education" of American youth under Federal Government control, removing the local influence of those most interested in ensuring they be as well educated as possible to succeed in life, placed their minds under control of those whose only concern is that Americans are not a threat to *"the Establishment,"* but to the extent possible, an extension of it, was the death knell for upward mobility and the future of a free and prosperous America.

Since that time those in control of the Federal Government have been in absolute control of the "education"/indoctrination of American youth.

***

Given the importance of this topic, if not **THE most important topic of this book,** it is appropriate to explore and expand on this subject that provided the foundation of America's 20th Century success and is at the root of the difference in the life of someone born in 1940, versus the lives of those born post 1960.

The following on this subject was published, in part, in 2003 in *"Connecting the Dots of American Politics."*

"Placid governability"

In America 2016 "education" is a misnomer. Indoctrination is closer to the truth, just as in Mao's People's Republic of China.

"American children, stuck in the government schools, and even in the universities, are being indoctrinated, much more than they are being educated.

"The *'Placid governability'* concept of the first President Bush's *"New World Order"* is preferable to American democracy, and David Rockefeller's *"excess of democracy"* comment connoting the *New World Order* disdain for democracy required rectification of the *"excess"* if the *New World Order* 'brains' were to achieve their greedy objectives.

"What better way to do this than emulate someone who was wildly successful in changing the direction of an entire country of one billion people, and who developed a method of controlling those masses by gaining control of the minds of all of the young who would eventually be the majority of the masses?

"To emulate Mao's success required gaining control of the means of indoctrination, the public school system, and converting it into the U.S. government system. But to gain control of such a large system required personnel in the form of many already inculcated with the ideas desirable to infuse into the young minds of America. This meant the universities producing those who would be the "teachers" of the young American minds would be the place to start.

"The 1993 edition of *Members of the Club* listed eight influential, universities with deans, professors, presidents, honorary fellows, or chancellors as members.

"Some of the prominent persons it showed associated with these universities, who might be recognizable were, in addition to Zbigniew Brzezinski; John Deutch, Harold Brown, Donna Shalala, George Schultz and Paul Volcker.

"With these highly placed people, who have also held senior Government positions, in such esteemed institutions of higher learning, the *'Establishment'* had more than its foot in the door of America's "education" system.

"Also, the White House, having been occupied by members for all but eight of the last forty years, and the President being the one who appoints the Secretary of Education has likely resulted in influence of note on the Government "education" system.

"The members who have been in both houses of the Congress, including ex-Speaker of the House, Thomas Foley, have had a hand in furthering 'the *Establishment'* cause of the 'education' program, and have had control of Government 'education' money that is never distributed without 'strings.'

"Members of various, 'liberal,' influential 'think' tanks, such as the Brookings Institution have conveyed their message throughout Government and media and have a strong influence in academia.

"Lastly, but certainly not the least influential person who has been a member, and would have helped cast a very long shadow over those indoctrinating the young minds of America, was Albert Shanker, President of the American Federation of Teachers.

"Has '*the Establishment*' through all of this influence been successful in replicating Mao's China success in America?

"An important <u>Insight</u> magazine article documents how U.S. public schools continue to develop as a tool for the left-wing to condition American school children to accept dependence and servitude...<u>Yes, the cultural Marxists have a plan for America</u>...poorer families have no choice but to accept whatever is handed out by the failed public school system...a huge new generation of docile, ignorant adults will emerge-much to the detriment of liberty in the United States. Even on U.S. university campuses, many administrations now require students to herd themselves into designated 'free-speech' zones before they are allowed to talk without restrictions on content."

-The American Sentinel, April 2002

"According to Ann Coulter, writing in HUMAN EVENTS, June 18, 2001, *'It is simply taken for granted that it's desirable for children to revere 'authority figures' at government schools...Children must be taught to love Big Brother, welcoming him to take over our schools, our bank accounts, our property...'*

"How could this have happened in America, the 'land of the free and the brave,' the country that has been a bastion of capitalism and democracy; that has provided a beacon for those desiring to experience the liberty and democracy it has offered for over two hundred years?

"Schools Training Cultural Soldiers, Not Teachers"

"Imagine that Dan Rather is your son's history teacher, Barbra Streisand teaches your daughter's English class, and Jane Fonda serves as the school's guidance counselor. Yes, it really is that bad. - Robert Ortiz, Ed. M., Harvard University 2001.

"Mr. Ortiz, being a recent graduate of the Harvard Graduate School of Education, HGSE, can provide, as well as anyone, real knowledge of how successful those desiring to destroy America's Capitalistic Western democracy through the Government indoctrination system have become. Writing in *HUMAN EVENTS*, in June 2001, he continued:

"As conservatives endeavor to reform public education, they will face stiff opposition from the very people with whom they entrust their policies -- and their children. Perched well to the left of American society, the nation's graduate schools of education have produced an educational establishment that considers itself to be on the front lines of the culture wars. Conservatives cannot afford to ignore the radical ideology and activist intentions of teacher education programs...Education schools not only lean radically leftward, but also equip their graduates to promote the liberal creed in American schools and classrooms... The academic course at HGSE resembles a casual luncheon with Ralph Neas and Martin Sheen. As Election Day neared last November, numerous classmates and even teaching fellows implored me to 'Pray that Gore wins!'...In my spring semester courses, students and faculty denounced conservatives easily and often as either stupid or dangerous or both...resplendent in its righteousness, HGSE (Harvard Graduate School of Education) precludes thoughtful debate by summarily excluding conservative views. Students regularly brand opponents of bilingual education as racists...the absence of conflicting viewpoints...encourages students and staff to believe that liberalism represents the only reasonable vision of a just society...defines itself through opposition to concepts of Euro-centrism, competition, patriarchy, and heterosexism. Courses rest on foundational assumptions that racism is rampant and gender is socially constructed, and prospective teachers debate the best way to teach adolescents these fundamental truths...Students and staff generally cite the under-representation and misunderstanding of minority experiences as the fundamental problem of American education...From this philosophy emerges a radical egalitarianism that values personal experience and cultural affirmation over skill acquisition and content knowledge...Dialects like Ebonics are not wrong; they illustrate the oppressiveness of a 'hidden curriculum.'...standardized evaluation, and reward systems are all rejected out of hand because they are believed to reinforce

society's racist, sexist, and capitalist structures...the centerpiece of HGSE's annual student research conference was a panel discussion that seriously asked, 'Cuban Education: Our Role Model?"

"Mr. Ortiz experienced a speech at the HGSE, on the role of arts in education, by Bill Ivy, the Clinton-appointed chairman of the National Endowment for the Arts, in which Mr. Ivy said, the arts *"are more important than reading and math...I believe in the message, and I will use any weapon in the arsenal."*

"This comment from the head of the Government agency responsible for fostering the arts in America, having been appointed by the President, member of ["the Establishment], is right out of the communist handbook.

"There is in fact no such thing as art for art's sake"
- Mao Tse-Tung

"With the chairman of the National Endowment for the Arts spouting Maoist philosophy for the education of America's children and the Harvard Graduate School of Education promoting the Cuban Communist "education" system that is also right out of Communist Mao's handbook, anyone attempting to determine the future of America should not have to look any deeper into the Government's system for indoctrinating the children of America to understand the true nature of America's "schools."

"Every concerned American should very seriously consider Mr. Ortiz' final cautions regarding American classrooms and teacher training; that teachers *"...so casually link conservatism to such undeniable evils as racism and the Holocaust."* And, *"Education schools are not teaching teachers to teach; they are training cultural soldiers. With an estimated 2-3 million teaching jobs opening up in the next decade, conservatives must either take teacher education seriously or, for the foreseeable future, concede our classrooms to activist liberalism."*

"There is no doubt *"activist liberalism"* is a euphemism for anti-capitalism, anti-Western American culture, pro-Socialist indoctrination. The "liberals" are bringing American education down in flames. <u>And every concerned American should be yelling, *"FIRE!"* loudly enough for Trump to hear them and get off his "ass" as he told Americans to do when encouraging them to vote.</u>

"Ignoring the schools turning out the '*cultural soldiers*' one has to look no further than the President of the United States to see the effectiveness of 'the Establishment' *New World Order* Socialist training programs.

"*Leftist*" Clinton '*loathed*' the military. Bush deliberately (hopefully) adopted a proletarian manner of speech to belie his real, North East, aristocratic background. Both are products of Yale at a time programs advancing the *New World Order* were just getting off the ground during their days there.

And both unmistakably advanced this same political agenda on domestic and international fronts. Most Americans are either confused or lulled into complacency by the fact Bush is a [veneer] Republican. But, make no mistake about it; he accomplished much of the agenda Clinton could not because he was a Democrat."

As did Barack Obama because he, as well as the first Bush, the second one and Clinton were all dancing to the pulling of their strings by the same Brzezinski anti-American... the "America" in which many of us grew up... puppet master who controlled and enriched all of them at the expense of the American people, and will continue to do so through Presidents who follow because it was not... until, possibly, Donald J. Trump... possible to become President of the United States without having been baptized into the religion of their Anti-American, *"Establishment"* *New World Order*, One World Government that is approaching the beginning of its fifth decade of... sorry, but there is no better, more concise, or articulate way of expressing what these evil people are continuing to do... f***ing up the entire world.

On that note, it is important to point out the fact of no perceptible difference in the method utilized, and in effect, between *"leftists,"* *"liberals,"* "Communists," "Fascists," "Marxists," and "the Establishment" *faux* "two party" political machine in control of America through its two veneers, "Democrats" and "Republicans."

So, no one should get "hung up" on the references to "Marxism" and "*Liberalism*" in the foregoing. It is only important to understand all the above are only slightly variant political concepts utilized to empower those in government at the expense of the masses, including the two superficial American political parties that are nothing more than contrivances to cause the ignorant members of the electorate to think they have a choice where there is none.

Little do they know as followers of each, they are merely being stupefied into believing there is a difference while both parties do nothing but serve *"the Establishment"* destructive powers behind the U.S. Government represented by the <u>faces</u> of Hillary and Bill Clinton, the Bushes, Obama and so many more, including TV "talking heads" trotted out daily to lie to them.

They have no idea they are fallen victim to one of the oldest power grab concepts in history: *"divide and conquer."*

All of the political concepts stated above, even if not originally intended as such, due to the insatiable desire for power of the nature of those who seek government as their refuge, eventually evolve as totalitarian political concepts whose adherents abhor free thinking. Thus, indoctrination into their way of "thinking" is their foundation for control.

The ultimate consequences… and objective… of all of these variously named forms of government and political thought is elimination of free thought among the masses, and implementation of totalitarianism, which is not unique to "Marxism," *"liberalism,"* "Fascism" or any of the other political concepts.

It is the *"Placid governability"* concept employed by each that should be important to everyone.

<u>Indoctrination via the "education" system is the foundation upon which all totalitarian governments are built because it is the thinking person who is a threat to his government.</u>

Thus, indoctrinating people, imbuing them with desired doctrines, lies, and contrived "facts" rather than encouraging them to analyze and think things out for themselves eliminates a lot of thinking among the masses detrimental to the goals and objectives of the government. The result of that diminution of thinking results in *"Placid governability."*

> ***"If you tell a lie big enough and keep repeating it, people will eventually come to believe it. The lie can be maintained only for such time as the state can shield the political, economic and/or military consequences of the lie. It thus becomes vitally important for the state to use all of its powers to repress dissent, for the***

truth is the mortal enemy of the lie and thus by extension, the truth is the greatest enemy of the state."
> - Joseph Goebbels, Hitler's Propaganda Minister

How can the state *"shield the political, economic and/or military consequences of the lie"*? This quote, also from Goebbels, should answer that: *"Think of the press as a great keyboard on which the government can play."*

Just insert the word "media" for *"press"* and think about the Government being at play with your mind the next time you are watching CNN, HLN, MSNBC, CNBC, or the network "news" on ABC, NBC or CBS. Then think about the fact that, as Propaganda Minister, Goebbels had complete control of all forms of media during Hitler's rein in Germany, and he was provided a large budget to ensure only what the state desired the people to know was disseminated through films, magazines, books, radio broadcast... the available forms of media at the time.

Today, in America, we have the FCC, Federal Communications Commission, a Government agency that has the power to revoke licenses of broadcast companies or stations, and thus function much like a Propaganda Minister, which they do.

Couple that with the fact Hitler's rise to power was facilitated by the hard economic times of the Great Depression and Goebbels' comments those hard times facilitated his getting the media of his day to become party to *"shield[ing] the political, economic and/or military consequences of the lie"* from the German people.

Barrack Obama's, untruths about the economy, unemployment, inflation, reasons for attacking Libya and removing Muammar Gaddafi, and more that will eventually be disclosed as the lies they were, were hammered into the heads of Americans seven days a week by "news" people who are willful liars for *"the Establishment"* they either know is destroying the freedom and rights of the people and any hope of a bright future, or they are young enough to have been indoctrinated into believing in their America destroying goals and objectives.

Either way these are just a few examples of what only the worst kind of people... the most-evil ones... could be part of in a Government that is doing what is being done to "America" and its people, or be extensions of that Government by being the keys on the *"great keyboard on which the government can play"* its lies of destruction. It is partially through perpetuation of falsehoods by the media upward mobility has been inhibited.

> ***"How fortunate for governments that the people they administer don't think."***   - Adolph Hitler

The American public school system inhibits upward mobility because *"poorer families have no choice but to accept whatever is handed out by the failed public school system"* that has eliminated education and imbuing youngsters with knowledge and the ability to be free thinkers in favor of indoctrination that enhances Government power rather than empowering the individual. Thus, a majority of our youth reach adulthood having had their intellectual legs cut out from under them before they have a chance.

Then they and their ever increasing *"huge new generation[s] of docile, ignorant adults"* form sort of a "glass ceiling" for everyone, limiting upward mobility from the top down through self-serving imposition of reverence for *"authority figures,"* which serves to impede free thinking as in Mao's China.

There, Mao Tse-Tung who was in total control of China's population for almost three decades at the time of his death in the mid-1970s and had written **"...we must constantly carry on lively and effective political education among the masses..."** i.e., indoctrination, was revered... as has happened in many cultures throughout history, and his political concept of Communism was as revered by the youth of China as he was.

Minus the single "Authority Figure," America is not far behind 1970s China on its road to totalitarianism. Americans better wake up and watch out now before it is too late.

The nature of the failed American "education"/indoctrination system in impeding upward mobility has played its part in the destruction of the American Middle Class and causing America to be more divided... structured along socioeconomic cultural lines.

And let's not forget that *"elite"* Harvard University has been at the forefront of the destruction of U.S. education for well over two decades, as demonstrated in Mr. Ortiz' words above.

***

Those with the financial means spend a lot to keep their children out of the hands of the public-school system. Their children… especially those of the so-called *"elite"* are educated in private institutions that prepare them for private universities that give them an intellectual leg up on life, rather than cutting their intellectual legs out from under them.

The difference in education of the majority and those from higher rungs of the socioeconomic ladder is comparable to the difference in the military indoctrination of draftee or volunteer enlisted men and that of the Officer Corps, which is vastly different.

But who would know. Few of the enlisted ever know the difference between their lot in life and that of an Officer. The abyss between the two lives is wide and deep, and few are equipped to cross it.

Ditto: the abyss between the lives of products of the American Government indoctrination system and those with private school and private university educations, as youth in America under the control of "*the Establishment*" following the guidance of Hillary, Obama or other Brzezinskites in control of their future also will never know.

<u>Take **"control of what people read and listen to and what children learn in school,"** has been followed since soon after Jimmy Carter entered the Oval Office in 1977.</u>

STEP FOUR: "DIVIDE AND CONQUER"

CREATING "DIVERSITY" THROUGH IMMIGRATION TO ENHANCE THE POWER OF THE GOVERNMENT OVER THE PEOPLE

It has been proven over and over again, and again in contemporary times *"diversity"* is not strength. Northern Ireland, Belgium, Spain, Yugoslavia, Czechoslovakia, the Middle East have all proven the divisiveness of culture, language and religion. That *"diversity"* is actually a weakness. It is disruptive to the peace and harmony of any place in which there are large, culturally different segments of population… as is being proven in America in 2016.

However, even with this knowledge *"the Establishment"* has long been working to do whatever it takes to ensure a strengthening of its position within this country. Their *"Diversity is our strength"* program has been a pivotal part of that endeavor, continuously indoctrinating young minds with this in the schools and older Americans through the media.

They are fully aware of the old adage *"divide and conquer,"* and have been assiduously pursuing division of America… to *"conquer"* in the literal sense of the word; to overcome, to defeat the people of America… for a half century as of 2016.

A divided America, one wherein there is cultural, racial, language and religious strife serves to strengthen the Government. A government that is, clearly, no longer a *"government of the people, by the people, for the people."* It is a government of, by and for those in power and those whom those in power serve.

The cultural, racial, religious and language division of America for the purpose of strengthening the Government over the people conceptualized by those behind the Government was put into active operation under President Jimmy Carter who was either totally complicit or terribly out of touch with reality, and naïve.

Thus it was during the Carter Administration restrictions on receipt of welfare, food stamps and other benefits to illegal aliens were lifted resulting in an immediate increase in the flow of illegal aliens from Mexico, people who are racially, culturally, religiously, linguistically different from the majority population of America; people who, prevalent in large numbers, would *"divide"* the country.

This effort has proven successful in accomplishing this in subsequent years.

Carter's signing of the Refugee Act of 1980 in March of that year opened the floodgates of illegal immigration from Mexico by providing for *"placement for economic self-sufficiency, cash assistance"* and covering the estimated cost at that time of $4,000 each for *"distribution to the states"* of the immigrants, spreading them among the population for *"diversity"* purposes.

Carter also had an "open arms" policy toward Cuban immigrants who were immediately granted refugee status. But that was apparently insufficiently aggressive in the plan to further expand a divisive population segment.

Between April and October of 1980 Carter cooperated with Cuban dictator Fidel Castro in shipping one hundred twenty-five thousand Cubans, many of questionable background, to the U.S. and granting them "refugee" resident status.

He employed the U.S. Coast Guard, Navy, Marines and Army in that five and one-half month effort to get all those Cubans into and settled in the U.S.

To see one, "little" result of that effort, all one must do is go to the West Lake, Lafayette Park area of Los Angeles where many of these "refugees" were settled.

This area of beautiful parks, once utilized by the people of Los Angeles, upscale shopping and affluent residential areas was turned into the most crime ridden, Rampart Division area serviced by the Los Angeles Police Department. The parks have chain link fences around them. They are closed at night. Shopping is gone.

The whole area is a crime infested, gang war combat zone, as has happened in many American cities… large and small… since.

But many years before this the U.S. Government, also under a Democrat, Lyndon Johnson, implemented immigration that when combined with this action created *"diversity"* problems they were possibly not sufficiently astute to foretell.

It was more Government stupidity gone wild at the expense of the taxpayers and less future harmony in the country that was going to be done without regard to the consequences, if anyone in the Government was sufficiently bright to consider, which is doubtful, or it was part of the *"diversity"* for power plan. Intent, or not, we will never know, but we do know the results.

It was just months… officially less than a full year… into the Vietnam War, which shows it was going badly almost from the beginning, as most involved or receiving reports from family and friends on the ground there were reporting from Vietnam.

Thousands of indigenous people were being brought to the U.S. purportedly for their safety because they were known allies of the U.S. military that invaded and was wreaking destruction for no discernable reason. They were being resettled all over the U.S. No one except those doing this knew the criteria for this, but whatever it was, relatively small cities were on the list.

Some of those being resettled in the U.S. as a result of the war were the Laotian Hmong people from along the Vietnam border who were not viewed favorably by the indigenous Vietnamese even before the arrival of the U.S. military.

These and the Vietnamese were village people who lived in huts with dirt floors and had never seen indoor plumbing or cooking over anything but a fire. (We should note this expensive and destructive stupidity has not ceased. Four decades later it was Somalis that were being given this "free ride.")

The Housing and Urban Development agency, HUD, was given responsibility to resettle these people in at least one small predominately homogenous city, and probably in others like it.

It is not known what they did elsewhere, but in this city of about fifty thousand the agency went into the poorer white parts of town, condemned houses as not fit for habitation, tore some down, remodeled others and created new immigrant neighborhoods.

After the houses were remodeled, they were "sold" to the immigrants for one dollar. They also built new houses at taxpayer expense on some of the lots where houses were torn down and "sold" those to the immigrants for a dollar also. But that was not the worst abuse of the taxpayers by the government in this program

Because these people did not know how to live in houses with bathrooms and kitchens, while their free housing was being readied for them, the government set up schools on how to utilize and take care of their new bathrooms and kitchens, and paid them $125, over $1,000 in 2016 dollars, per week to go to "school" to learn this. Essentially, they were being paid by the taxpayers to learn how to cook and go to the bathroom.

After the Vietnamese were taken care of HUD, for self-preservation, as Government agencies are inclined, began to take care of the relatively small numbers of Mexican immigrants at the time, before Carter's Refugee Act, also at taxpayer expense when the programs were expanded to the growing Latino community.

That required spending as much as fifteen thousand dollars per house for upgrades and repairs they could not afford out of their welfare checks they were receiving while they were, according to reports of some familiar with the program, watching TV as others were being paid by taxpayers to repair and upgrade their homes.

Remember: this was a predominately homogenous small city of fifty thousand. Guess what happens to a town that size after a few years growth of two diverse ethnic populations like Vietnamese and Latinos competing for the largesse and drug selling territories.

We don't have to guess. We have seen it growing all over the U.S. for over four decades. Since the 1970s, this ethnic *"diversity"* has resulted in increased violence, gang warfare, and tremendous economic and social cost. There are Asian, Latino and black gangs engaged in armed conflict on the streets of America… thanks to the stupidity of empirically disproven, *"diversity is a strength,"* U.S. Government policies.

1998, the subject city had a population of over 150 thousand that was 29% white, 20% black, 43% Latino and 8% Asian.

An interview with a funeral home owner still operating the funeral home his family owned in the 1950s when he was in high school told that over half the funerals he was conducting in the 1990s were for Vietnamese and Mexican males under the age of thirty killed by gunfire. Yep; *"diversity is strength."*

The worst abuse of the taxpayer citizens by *"the Establishment"* resulting from idiotic *"diversity"* programs continuing to be imposed on towns and cities that continued in 2016 is the deliberate destruction of the previous relative peace and harmony of homogenous populations, social and educational decline, and tremendous concomitant economic costs, as well as loss of life "*Liberal progressive*" members of *"the Establishment"* like Hillary and Obama are hell bent on continuing with more Latin immigration, plus Islamic immigrants of questionable intent.

This is another of those "*Establishment*" Government created problems of which anyone smart enough to make his or her way into Congress could not possibly be unaware. Thus, this destruction of towns and cities all over America through civil strife and the economic cost of it must be deliberate.

It is the classic *"divide and conquer,"* weaken the population and create a greater need for more government. There is no other explanation for this imposed *"diversity"* in small towns and cities all over America. But it must stop if "America" is to survive, if it is not too late.

Based on their stated positions, only one of the two 2016 Presidential candidates would endeavor to stop this idiocy, the other, preying on the ignorance of her primary constituency guaranteed she would continue the program, most detrimental to her base simply due to the prospect of continued socialism for their segment of the population, which is shortsighted on the part of the candidate, as well as detrimental to the population she represents.

She cannot ever be forgiven for this continued destruction.

ILLEGAL IMMIGRATION
"United States shall protect each of them
[states] *against invasion."*
Article IV Section 4.
Constitution of the United States

Because of past actions by the Mexican military and federal police on the U.S./Mexican border against the U.S. and U.S. citizens, the U.S. Congress has the authority to place the U.S. military on the border to treat Mexican nationals crossing the border as enemies of the United States.

Further, in addition to this power provided in the U.S. Constitution, the questions about Mexican illegal immigrants "rights" are moot. They can, and should be, arrested and detained, which they could be anyway, if the laws, rather than political correctness, were being enforced, since, by definition, they are breaking the law by illegally entering the U.S.

Although the illegal immigrants probably do not think of their entering the U.S. as invading with a vision of conquest, or make a Latin inroad against Western culture, it is clearly their intent to intrude upon, infringe, and even plunder the U.S. healthcare, welfare, education and social security systems.

The Mexican military and federal police, on the other hand, have definitely, consciously and deliberately, made armed incursions into the U.S., wherein it was their intent, through the use of armed force, to impose themselves and their illegal activities upon America and American citizens, and they violated the rights, and endangered the lives of U.S. border patrol agents on the U.S. side of the border.

Thus they have invaded.

Entering with a view to conquest and make a Latin inroad against American culture may not be in the minds of illegal immigrants, even though many demonstrate that after here, but it is implicit in the words of Mexican officials who refer to illegal immigration of their nationals into the U.S. as *"natural migration."*

They have refused to recognize the sovereignty of the United States and rather than endeavoring to prevent illegal immigration of their citizens, have a policy of encouraging it. This policy was echoed by the ranking Mexican government representative in Los Angeles in stating Californians should just accept the Mexicans are there to stay.

The political elite in Mexico have a reason for wanting their less fortunate citizens to leave their country.

Of the over one hundred million citizens of Mexico forty percent live in poverty. The economic system and culture in Mexico, even with the industrialization resulting from NAFTA created jobs cannot adequately provide for these forty million.

The per capita Gross Domestic Product of Mexico is one seventh of that of the U.S. with a third of the population. And the Latin Church, the dominant cultural institution in Mexico, has a policy that is not in the best interest of these Mexican people. The Pope suggested, during his last visit, he would prefer to see more, rather than fewer, Mexican members of his church there.

Contrary to the politically correct message of the U.S.

Government indoctrination system and Washington politicians, Mexico is not a democracy. Its form of government is an oligarchy wherein very few citizens have political power.

It is not a government of, for, or by, the people. It a government of the few, by the few, for the few, in which it is exceedingly difficult for the average citizen to move up the socioeconomic ladder... as is becoming the situation in *"the Establishment"* controlled America.

The oligarchy have little interest in instituting reforms that would change the country to a more democratic one, and even if they did, it is doubtful the change would take hold quickly enough to provide the needed benefits because of the nature of the people, the extent of the role of the Church in their lives, and the sheer magnitude of forty million uneducated, poor people, unqualified to contribute to the country's advancing economic prosperity.

This more religious, indigenous segment of the population is the poorest, least educated, and potentially most volatile. This means the country has forty million potential rebels, some with Communist proclivities... on the U.S. southern border, not unlike Cuba pre1960 with its also strongly U.S. supported President. But there is not a body of water between the U.S. and Mexico.

Rather than deal with this segment of the population, the oligarchs prefer to get rid of their problem by sending them to the U.S. where they can become the problem of Americans, and will send much of the money they make in the U.S. back home to help their families remaining in Mexico: a win-win situation for the oligarchs, but a losing proposition for America.

In the real world, if that concept exists in Washington D.C., the U.S. Government would act to protect interests of the country and its taxpayers as it is constitutionally charged with the responsibility to.

It would stop illegal immigration, put the Mexican Government on notice its policies, actions of some of its personnel and the effect of these actions on citizens of the U.S. qualify Mexico as an invading enemy of the United States.

This is serious. *"The Establishment"* should not permit Mexico to solve its problem by moving it to the United States. But they are smarter than Presidents and Government of the U.S. and they are not subject to political correctness.

Also <u>the Mexicans have a symbiotic relationship with *"the Establishment"* political whores in the U.S. Government. They desire to get rid of the least desirable and least productive members of their population to enhance the finances and future of their country while the political whores in the U.S. desire exactly the opposite. They want them here to weaken the productive population to strengthen their Government positions.</u>

***

Although Mexico has only a roughly thirty-five hundred dollar per capita Gross Domestic Product that is only one seventh of that of the U.S., the average per capita GDP of the Central American countries immediately South of Mexico is just one quarter of that.

So, to those people Mexico looks pretty good and they have a desire to engage in its northward, *"natural migration."* However, this is where the Mexican oligarchy prefers to depart from the U.S. fiction and have real world, pragmatic policies.

Mexico stops the *"natural migration"* of Central Americans at its southern border and detains them unless they are those being guaranteed safe passage into the U.S. as desired by *"the Establishment"* for "more *diversity."*

The Mexican government supports its ridiculous, insulting, concept of *"migration"* only when it benefits them by getting those deemed undesirable out of their country. This makes them hypocrites on the order of the U.S. Government *"Establishment."*

Some Americans may envisage *"migration"* as the migratory flights of birds wandering back and forth, from North to South, on a seasonal basis, rather than the fact the illegal immigrants are moving into the U.S. to take up permanent residence with the encouragement of Hillary, Obama and the rest of *"the Establishment"* to fulfill their *"divide and conquer"* plans to empower themselves over Americans.

There is nothing natural about illegal invasion of foreign nationals across a border into a sovereign nation. What is happening is patently unnatural. And the Mexican government demonstrates it knows this through its actions on its own Southern border.

Mexican nationals are unnaturally, illegally immigrating into the U.S. because of an acquired taste for U.S. Dollars, free schools, welfare, food stamps, Social Security payments, and free healthcare available to them, but not to taxpaying Americans with assets to lose. They are seeking these benefits in the U.S. because, due to the forty percent poverty rate in their non-productive, biased, Oligarchy culture, they are not available in Mexico.

Once these immigrants are here, have "tasted" these benefits, and the ease with which they can obtain them, they are not going back to Mexico. And those in the U.S. Government charged with the responsibility to enforce the laws have demonstrated, because of political correctness, they are not going to enforce immigration laws against minority immigrants. They are more concerned about political correctness than about the law, or the health, safety and welfare of taxpaying American citizens whom it is their desire to further subdue through their *"diversity"* program.

American citizens would be arrested, fined and even imprisoned for doing what millions of illegal immigrants are doing every day. They are stealing from the U.S. Government and by extension from U.S. taxpayers by illegally obtaining welfare benefits with the use of fraudulent documents and failing to pay income taxes when working for cash. They are also stealing from American taxpayers by being here illegally, and obtaining the benefits of schools, jobs and healthcare that are rightfully benefits of only those legal residents of the country who pay for them through their taxes.

There are tens of thousands of Mexicans living along the U.S. border who are stealing these benefits without even immigrating into the U.S. They obtain welfare benefits through the use of fraudulent documents, obtain a U.S. post office box address, have the checks mailed to the box, and come across the border to pick up their checks, or to obtain free healthcare.

Arizona is referred to as the health maintenance organization, HMO, for Mexico. The U.S. government is aware of this, but does nothing. Thus, the U.S. Government is condoning the theft of taxpayer funds by foreign nationals at the same time its position is that certain benefits for American citizens are not affordable.

Mexican nationals come into the U.S. to have their babies for free. Some estimates are citizens living in areas where there are large numbers of illegal immigrants are paying for as many as seven when they go into the hospital to have one baby. But these people are not a drain on the American taxpayer just because of the cost of having their babies in U.S. hospitals.

A baby born in the U.S. is an American citizen. And since U.S. immigration policy favors families of U.S. citizens, the new U.S. citizen has the right to have his or her family with him or her.

It would not make sense to say the citizen baby could not have its mother or father with it, but this is not where it ends. The new citizen's entire family will probably be permitted to immigrate.

Even the grandparents who have never paid a penny into Social Security may come to the U.S., retire, and draw Social Security benefits. (Let an American citizen who has not qualified attempt to obtain Social Security. It is a crime!)

Mexican government officials have openly articulated a policy of complete disregard for U.S. laws and sovereignty. They are actively promoting their Mexican invasion for their economic and peace at home benefits previously stated.

Most of the Washington politicians from both sides of the aisle seem to be going along with this politically correct displacing of America's Western culture, and eventual destruction of great swaths of American prosperity, by doing nothing to stop illegal immigration, and by lying to the American public about false *"advantages"* of it.

It is obvious the foolish *"liberal, progressive"* veneer of *"the Establishment"* are doing this to broaden their power base, but is it possible veneer Republicans are so intellectually challenged they actually believe they can convert Mexicans to Republicans, or is there something more sinister in their position?

It should be obvious to anyone who can read or has a television there is no positive, no advantage to Mexican immigration legal or illegal.

The obvious differences between American and Latin cultures and the immigrants' demonstrated resistance to assimilation and adopting the English language should be enough warning to everyone that millions of Mexican Nationals bringing their culture and language to the U.S. cannot, in any way, be positive for the future of any American citizens.

With total disregard of the empirical evidence of the adverse impact of Mexican immigration "*the Establishment*" and its "*liberal, progressive*" members, through their mouthpiece media like the *NEW YORK TIMES,* and so called "*liberal*" think tanks continue to promote advantages of Mexican immigration.

They say the immigrants do jobs other Americans are unwilling to do, and even advocate *"ordinary, illegal, otherwise law-abiding immigrants"* should not be arrested by state or local law enforcement agencies.

This is what everyone should expect from the non-"thinking" so called "*liberal*s" who erroneously consider themselves "*elite.* "

This amounts to selectively enforcing laws, or not enforcing laws, based on the ethnicity of individual lawbreakers. They are now demonstrating the form of Government they would like to see in America would subjectively determine which laws are to be enforced, and against whom.

The logical progression of this type of "thinking" would lead to selectively enforcing, or not enforcing, laws based upon against whom a crime is perpetrated. (Look for this next.) What is it they do not understand about "illegal"?

How about this? Inform local law enforcement agencies they are not to arrest *"ordinary ... otherwise law-abiding ..."* citizens who trespass, break and enter, commit fraud against American citizens, companies, or the Government by illegally obtaining welfare or other benefits, cheat on their taxes, etc.

C'mon! The laws must either be enforced against all who break them without regard to ethnicity, origin, religion, or citizenship, or they must be taken off the books. A democracy requires impartiality in the administration of justice.

The *"liberal, progressive"* members of "*the Establishment*" like Hillary Clinton, Obama and their media mouthpieces who every time they open their mouths show how really stupid they are fully understand what they are doing.

They are endeavoring to destroy American democracy, and replace it with their Brzezinski, fictional "1984," "Brave New World" Utopian, Socialist vision their lack of common sense and real world experience cause them to believe is actually possible contrary to available empirical facts.

***

Remember, they "think" they are in charge, and the Government they desire that would be consistent with their Socialist views and those of every oligarchy and dictatorship in the world... including the multiplicity of failed ones... permits the few in charge to determine what the laws are and against whom they are applied.

This is the reason they promote the immigration of millions who have never experienced the democracy they desire to deprive Americans of with such avidity.

<u>These people are exactly the types John Adams warned America about when he wrote:</u> ***"Our Constitution was made only for a moral and religious people. It is wholly inadequate to the government of any other."***

When anyone reads, in publications like *THE NEW YORK TIMES,* arguments against moral clarity, it is selective application of laws, morals, ethics and values for which they are arguing.

And regarding the nonsense about immigrants *"doing jobs other Americans won't.* This is just more *"liberal, progressive"* hogwash!

If welfare were eliminated for those mentally and physically capable of working and earning a living, they would do those jobs the immigrants are doing when they are young, learn the benefits of working, progress up the income scale, AND the culture of dependency, drugs and crime, those supporting illegal immigration and welfare are directly responsible for, would be dealt a healthy blow to the benefit of all Americans, especially black Americans about whose self-esteem these same *"liberal, progressives"* and "educators" express so much concern.

Mexican immigration is particularly unhealthy for the circumstances and self-esteem of black Americans.

All black Americans should reconsider their position of siding with the other major minority against America's Western culture they erroneously define as "white."

They have been "sucked into" this position by the *"leftist, liberal progressives"* through their denigrating "pitching" of the benefits of a culture of dependency to those they perceive susceptible because of the legacy of their African culture. And they have done this, not to benefit black Americans, but to broaden their power base. But Black Americans, most of whom can trace their "Americanism" back a minimum of five generations; have much more in common with white Americans than with Latino immigrants, including language and religion, the two most significant elements of all cultures.

As previously stated, black Americans have always been part of American culture. It has been only recently the *"liberal, progressives"* on their *"divide and conquer"* for power mission of weakening the United States internally have marketed a contrived African culture to black Americans.

They are deliberately exploiting the natural, inherent cultural imperative of black Americans to "belong" to African culture just as they are in cahoots with Mexico in exploiting those of Latin culture for the same purpose.

The cultural imperative is visceral, not intellectual. But cultural adherence can be mental. When people are not bound by geographic or governmental constraints and free to choose, as Americans are, they may choose to view the world through the cultural options available. The key word being, "choose."

Therefore, black Americans, being citizens of the U.S. having all the rights and privileges of citizenship can, as many have, choose to fully participate in their American Western culture, or they can reverse the progress they have made, and adopt a mythical African cultural mindset to their own detriment.

<u>Should black Americans choose to continue to permit themselves to be used by their African-like, despotic "leadership," and *"liberal, progressives"* as a part of their power base in their anti-Western culture support of illegal immigration they will be the ones to suffer the most among all residents of America.</u>

Black Americans should ask: can we commit the same illegal infractions as illegal immigrants and expect the same people calling for suspension of law enforcement against them do the same for us? But never mind. The prisons attest the answer: no!

They should also be cognizant of the fact language and religion are the two most divisive cultural characteristics. Then they should consider that in the decade between the 1990 and 2000 census, because of illegal immigration the population of Latinos in America grew to equal that of blacks and fifty percent of all those of Latin heritage in the U.S. were foreign born, this illegal immigration is not subsiding, and likely by 2016 major areas of the

U.S. a large percentage of black Americans call home have become home to majority Latino, Spanish speaking, Latin Church populations that tend to be culturally intolerant, and favor less free, socialist, or dictatorial forms of government.

Further, in 2016, over fifty percent of the Spanish speaking population gets its news solely from Spanish language media.

In 2002, the estimated nine million Spanish speaking illegal immigrants living in America were only equal to about twenty five percent of the entire black population, and were taking jobs and benefits that would otherwise be available if not for illegal immigration being fostered by those individuals who also purport to be advocates for them.

In many states, the Latino population has become so large the states are already being redistricted to provide more Latino backed representation in Congress.

<u>Black Americans should ask themselves whether they believe their circumstances would be better when living under a culturally cohesive, less tolerant, Spanish speaking, Latin majority than they are with a proven generous, compassionate, democratic, Protestant majority with which they share both language and religion.</u>

Then, they should ask those who advocate "African Americanism" today what they will be advocating when the Spanish speaking population numbers twice that of black Americans.

<u>Latin immigration is bad for all Americans, culturally and economically, but it is worse, near term, for Black Americans.</u>

Thus, they like all Americans should wake up to the reality of the situation rather than continue to listen to "*liberal, progressives*" who will sell them "*down the river*" whenever and wherever the numbers of the Spanish speaking population surpass their numbers. Political power which equals M-O-N-E-Y is the name of the game!

Waiting, rather than pragmatically looking at trends and the current real world situation and failing to take action to stop this immigration will result in a Latin American United States being *fait accompli.*

Any illegal immigrant who makes it across the border into the U.S., under the current Mexican government supporting mentality of most of "*the Establishment,*" is probably home free.

There are at least one million of these each year. But black Americans are not the only ones who should be concerned near term. Republicans and black Americans are in the same boat. Mexican immigration will be the end of the Republican veneer of the *faux* "two party" system and Western culture in America.

Thus, black Americans, the Western culture that affords them so much opportunity and the Republicans are on the losing end of Mexican immigration. The *"leftist, liberal, progressives"* will be the big winners because they will have a greatly expanded power base with a demonstrated, socialist proclivity.

"Liberal, progressives" in America will finally realize their heyday. Hell! Given they will have a large enough base of support with socialist proclivities to whom the appellation *"socialist"* does not carry any negative connotation they might just change their name to reflect their true identity as *NWO* communists.

But whether they change their name, it is a sure bet they will pander to and support the large Latin population culture in every way including language they will have to speak or be out of office.

The only winners will be immigrants and the new Socialist Party. Everyone else loses, even Americans of Latin heritage whose families have been Americans for generations.

As people are prone to do, they will paint these Americans with the same brush as the immigrants, even though many of them do not even speak Spanish.

Profiling may not be politically correct, but it is natural for people to associate others on the basis of appearance and observed conduct of the majority.

***

There is another fact of Mexican immigration of which all Americans should be cognizant. The U.S. is suffering a loss of highly paying manufacturing jobs at the same time it is absorbing a large, growing Third World population from the least desirable segment of the Mexican and Central American populations.

<u>The fact of this, despite illogical arguments to the contrary, is America and thus its population, is regressing. At a time when the Western world and even Mexico are advancing America is moving toward Third World status as its population of those of a Third World cultural mindset increases.</u>

Mexico is advancing solely as a result of U.S. jobs moved there under terms of NAFTA, and they represent advancement, not regression. It is NOT those capable of filling those manufacturing jobs that are "moving" into the U.S. It is the least well-educated, least capable to contribute who are *Coming to America.*

The Mexican government wants to get rid of those who would restrain Mexico's advancement. And, even though this advancement is gratis, compliments of America, it is Americans to whom it is more than willing to transfer its burden. Does this sound like friend, or foe?

That illegal immigrants are actually aliens, foreign in culture, and different in nature, although not politically correct, should be obvious. That large numbers of them are having an adverse effect on American civilization should also be obvious.

The United States, its civilization, like any country or functioning system is much like a large, living organism. It has, per Webster, *"diverse parts that function as a whole to maintain its life and its activities."*

An invader, as defined by Webster, is one who chooses to *"crowd into, throng, intrude upon, infringe, violate, to enter and spread through with harmful effects, to make an invasion."* The synonym of invade is trespass, *"go beyond the limits of what is right or moral, do wrong, transgress, unlawful entry upon the property or rights of another."*

These are words, terms and concepts appropriate for the discussion of illegal immigration and its effects on America.

As previously stated, unlike the Mexican government and its agents, it is probably not the cognitive intent of the illegal aliens to invade. They do not think of themselves as invading in the true sense of the word. But the consequences are nonetheless the same.

They are knowingly, willfully crowding into the U.S. in violation of U.S. laws. Much like any trespasser, they are deliberately and knowingly, infringing, violating, and unlawfully entering upon the property and rights of Americans.

Permitting the illegal aliens to knowingly violate U.S. law, to come into the country and go beyond the limits of what they, the aliens, know to be wrong without there being any consequences to them for this willful wrong doing will have severe, long term, negative consequences for Americans that cannot be overlooked.

This will result in an expansion of the numbers of the criminal class, and increased economic and social cost to the country beyond what has already happened that is extensive.

In California this is already obvious. Whereas only fourteen percent of the citizen population was on welfare, twenty one percent of the immigrants were drawing welfare benefits. And fifteen percent of the violent criminals in California prisons in 2000 were these immigrants.

The foreign, different nature of the immigrants cannot help but have an adverse effect upon the functioning American system, especially since they persist in speaking a language that is alien to this system, and they are accustomed to a different set of cultural values and a less free form of government.

The accommodation of non-English speaking millions is costly and dysfunctional to the otherwise smooth functioning of the American system. This can already be observed in schools and the provision of essential Government services.

According to *THE NEW YORK TIMES*, *"The number of students with limited English skills, most of them Hispanic, has doubled to five million in the last decade...more than four times the rate for the general population...We are now experiencing the largest wave of immigration in the history of the United States."* And, according to the U.S. census, this immigration is resulting in a decline in the median income of American cities.

The invasion of millions of aliens who know they are violators of the laws of the American system, who know their system encourages violation of American law, and who are intent on imposing their customs and cultural characteristics on America, rather than assimilating to derive the greater benefits of the American system, can do nothing except wreak havoc upon the American system. It is totally dysfunctional.

The invading aliens are a threat to the health and safety of Americans and to the integrity of the American system. They are a threat for the reasons cited above and because of their alien, Third World culture mentality.

***

The ultimate consequence of the unchecked, illegal invasion of Latin immigrants into the U.S. that will permit them to become

<u>the largest ethnic group will result in dissolution of the free, democratic, capitalistic and prosperous America that was developed by a Western, Protestant culture that is alien and uncomfortable to the invaders.</u>

If Mexico had a culture or a system anything like the American democratic, capitalistic system Mexican Nationals would not be leaving their country to come to America for what they perceive to be a better life. But it does not and cannot. The Mexican system is not capitalistic in that the availability of capital is extremely limited.

Without capital availability for small business investment and home purchases Mexico will never be able to provide a satisfactory, in the Western sense, standard of living for its population. And the oligarchs have never demonstrated any desire to help advance the welfare of their citizens in that regard. They prefer to place most of their capital in a safer environment than that they have wrought. They put their money in U.S. investments.

Although most are not cognizant of it, the nature of a country and its culture or system of government is a direct result of the mindset and characteristics of the people who comprise it.

Therefore, it is mandatory to consider what wrought the Mexican system the illegal aliens are leaving and that same system they will impose upon any part of America where they reach critical mass majority status.

To view this future America all anyone has to do is visit Los Angeles. Go downtown, or to the Wilshire District that was once so attractive and prosperous, prior to the massive Latin invasion of the area that turned it into a Latin, crime-ridden ghetto.

Then go to Mexico City where it is not safe to drive a nice car, wear a good watch, or take a taxi if you are a "gringo," to see the future of Los Angeles. Both of these experiences would be prophetic trips into the future of a Latin American United States.

"The Establishment liberal progressives" either desire to ignore or are incapable of intellectually grasping the empirical evidence of these adverse consequences of Mexican immigration. They think they will not be affected. They will be above it, and in charge, as did Hillary Clinton who so assiduously pursued turning America into Mexico.

This is short sighted on their part. But <u>average Americans, who will definitely be adversely affected in their everyday lives, should not overlook the consequences of what unchecked immigration holds for them, and should act to avert the future it will bring.</u>

<u>To save America, its form of government, culture, civilization, and provide a free, democratic and prosperous future for it, requires an immediate cessation of Mexican and Central American immigration</u>. But this will not happen unless sufficient numbers of American citizens become well enough informed to demand it.

***

Both the Mexican Government and "*the Establishment*" are fully cognizant of the negative impact upon America of its Mexican invasion even if the "*liberal, progressives*" life of privilege has sheltered them from these world realities.

The Mexican Government demonstrates knowledge of what the unchecked immigration of those from a less successful culture can do to the prosperity of a country by stopping Guatemalans, Hondurans, Salvadorans and Nicaraguans at its Southern border.

Too bad "*the Brzezinski Establishment*" in the U.S. wants what Mexico does not.

This policy to prevent adverse effect upon the prosperity of their country while, at the same time, enhancing its prosperity by having its least desirable citizens engage in northward, *"natural migration"* shows, unlike the U.S. Government, the Mexican Government is working for the benefit of those Mexicans who choose to remain in Mexico.

It is just not possible "*the Establishment*" of the U.S. Government cannot see and not understand what the Mexican Government is doing. It is working for the benefit of its country and its citizens who can contribute to its future, while those in successive U.S. Government Administrations have also been working for the benefit of Mexico and other interests who benefit from moving production to Mexico and importing cheap labor into the U.S. to the disadvantage of taxpaying Americans who are paying their salaries. Why?

Unfortunately, the answer always has to be M-O-N-E-Y. The U.S. government is not working to enhance the lot of the average working American. The last four U.S. Presidents clearly demonstrated they were working in accord with the Brzezinski Business Plan to enrich big business powerful interests that benefit most from production in Third World countries and Third World labor for production in America to secure their support for achievement of *New World Order* goals.

There is just not another answer. No one could actually be dumb enough to be unaware of the obvious consequences of the outflow of production <u>and</u> unchecked inflow of immigrants.

But, O.K! So U.S. Presidents and the rest of the U.S. Government have been working for economic interests other than those of the average taxpaying American. But permitting U.S. sovereignty to be physically attacked, and do nothing about it?

How could these Presidents of the United States get away with ignoring these attacks and calling the leaders of the country perpetrating them a *"friend"*?

Simple: <u>the controlled complicit U.S. media is the gate keeper that determines what information the American public is privy to.</u>

There have been over one hundred known incursions, invasions of the sovereign United States, by Mexican government military and federal police. Many of these occurred since George Bush was in office. On two of these occasions, in the fall of 2001, near El Paso, Texas, and in May 2002 in Arizona, U.S. Government Border Patrol officials were fired upon by the Mexican military.

During the incidents in May 2002, as reported by a U.S. congressman on the Bill O'Reilly show on the Fox News channel, the Mexican military intruded five miles into Arizona and shot out the windshield and a tire on the Border Patrol agent's vehicle.

Bill O'Reilly questioned why the U.S. media did not report this. This was a good question O'Reilly could have answered easily. <u>But the more important question is why would the President of the United States and his Administration permit hostile military incursions into the sovereign territory of the United States</u>, wherein the lives of U.S. government agents have been put at risk, without mentioning them, or taking actions to stop this conduct well before the occurrences reached over one hundred in number? <u>And having reached over one hundred, why are U.S. Presidents not only still</u>

silent on the subject, but still embracing the leaders of the government that perpetrated these actions against America?

The answer to that is also simple: because George Bush II just like his father who was a charter member was also a political whore for the anti-American *New World Order* his father Bush I proudly announced just twelve years prior to his son being put into the Brzezinski *"Establishment"* controlled Government for the benefit of almost everyone in the world except working taxpaying American citizens.

Also the Goebbels-like U.S. media would not report these incursions because it is also controlled by the same interests as both Bushes, and they did not want the American public to know what Mexicans are doing to America.

Bringing it to the attention of the average American citizen who might take more notice of an actual act of hostile invasion than of the media supported illegal immigration could raise a red flag that could result in an outpouring of negative opinion against Mexicans and their immigration, which would not have been good for the Brzezinski plan and its supporters like the Bushes.

This is just another media action, or inaction, that more than justifies the appellations crooked, biased, fake, plain dishonest, or anything we can think of because they are all accurate.

But it is a safe bet they would not have been silent if it had been the U.S. military venturing into Mexico in an effort to stop the illegal drug trade the Mexican incursions are supporting. They and their *"liberal, progressive"* friends would have made anti-U.S. military, pro-Mexican, media hay!

What was the policy of *"the Establishment"* Oval Office occupied by Bush and now Obama regarding protecting U.S. borders and citizens when a foreign country's police and military actually invade U.S. territory and fire on U.S. government agents?

Since the U.S. is supposedly engaged in its "War on Drugs," and the Mexicans are making their incursions in support of the Mexican drug runners who have strong ties to corrupt Mexican Government, military and police officials who benefit from the sale of illegal drugs in the U.S., should not these invasions be viewed in the context of the "War" just as the perpetrators of terrorism are viewed in the "War on Terror"?

To fail to put the U.S. military on the Mexican American border, and to pursue the Mexican invaders who attack U.S. citizens and property in the United States across the border into Mexico just as the U.S. is pursuing terrorists in the "War on Terror" half way around the world, is intellectually and operationally inconsistent.

It makes a joke of the "War on Drugs," and continues to send the wrong message to the President and citizens of Mexico that U.S. laws and sovereignty do not apply to any Mexicans whose desire it is to break them. Is this not, yet, another example of political correctness run amuck?

***

Let's see: U.S. agents operating inside Mexico in the drug "War" are not permitted to carry weapons for their own protection. Some have even been murdered by the Mexicans. Armed Mexican Government agents on the other side in this "War" can invade the U.S. over one hundred times, fire at U.S. government property and U.S. citizens with impunity, the media never reports it, and the President of the United States never mentions it, or does anything about it. Is this great policy (for Mexico) and great "Homeland Security," or what?

Boy! Mexican and U.S. Presidents must be <u>really</u> good friends or, at least, Presidents of the United States are better friends to Mexican Presidents than to the American public. Could it be in the titles? "American public" just does not seem to have the import of the titles of the two men. Nor do the policies of the U.S. support the import or the position and authority implied by "President."

Or, maybe, *the Establishment*" has visions of the greater political grandeur of the combined North American countries.

Whatever! The policies and lack of action make the "World's Only Superpower" a laughing stock to all Mexicans, especially drug cartels and everyone else in the world. They are also a disaster with regard to the impact of Mexican immigration, invasions, illegal drugs, and on the future of America.

The U.S. Government is supposedly conducting its "War on Drugs," and the President is the Chief Executive Officer of the Government agencies involved in the "War" as well as the Commander in Chief of the U.S. Military should utilize the full force of all law enforcement and the military in this "War" to stop the terrible damage it is doing to America. The large numbers of Americans dying as a result of drugs being brought over our southern border require and legally justify this.

Even though none of the recent Presidents or other politically connected members of their generation had even a passing acquaintance with the military, they should know the titles confer not just respect from others but an obligation to fulfill the roles the titles also confer.

Therefore when officials of a foreign government's agencies or military such as the Mexican National Police, or Mexican Military, invade U.S. territory and take hostile action, such as firing at U.S. citizens and property, this should trigger the Commander in Chief and the Chief Executive Officer of the United States, and the U.S. Congress, into action.

The fact the U.S. is engaged in "War" against those very elements perpetrating the attacks should elicit a prompt response from it. For the President and the Congress to ignore these attacks, to fail to address them, or act to prevent them, represents a failure to fulfill the responsibilities of the position the title connotes.

Also given the fact several U.S. Presidents previously created *false flag* events, lied to the American people, Congress and even the United Nations to start unnecessary wars then wasted trillions of dollars in these wars does it not make sense that when there is a real attack from a country actually adversely affecting the U.S., resulting in deaths of tens of thousands of Americans, at least one of these Presidents should have acted strongly against that country rather than against those that did nothing to deserve being attacked?

***

The following should prove what worthless political hacks, rather than protectors of Americans and their country, those Presidents, especially the most recent two, Bush II and Obama, were.

Also, in addition to these two; Clinton, Carter and Bush I were hacks who did nothing while in Office except serve their puppet master Brzezinski to further weaken the United States in pursuit of his ultimate NWO goals... proving the power of billions of dollars of Rockefeller money.

Note: <u>Article I Section 8. of the *Constitution of the United States* states</u>; ***"The Congress shall have Power to ... provide for*** *calling forth the Militia to ... repel Invasions."*

Article I Section 8. Also states, the Congress shall have the power *"To make all Laws which shall be necessary and proper for carrying into Execution the foregoing Powers."*

WELL? What the hell held back the most recent four Presidents and Congress from doing their duty to protect the American people as they are supposed to?

Answer: the damned *New World Order* of which all are either members or nothing but obedient little servants.

If Bush II had used the military to quell the invasions and drugs from Mexico instead of lying about "9/11" and Iraq, then invading, bombing and killing hundreds of thousands of people in the Middle East, the U.S. and Americans would have five trillion dollars less wealth depleting debt, thousands of us would still be alive, uninjured, Islamic terror would not have been dramatically ramped up by his wars, the Mexican immigration and drug problems of 2016 would not be with us, and Bush would be a hero rather than the International War Criminal he legitimately is.

But the failure of these Presidents and the U.S. Congress to take actions against Mexican Government invasions, by definition, is indicative of the problems plaguing the Government at ALL levels, in all three branches: incompetence and greed!

They are *bought and paid for* to satisfy the *NWO* plans for America, not to do what is in the best interest of Americans.

If these people were in private enterprise, or public companies, they would probably be fired for incompetence and negligence because it can easily be proven none of them are attempting to fulfill their obligations to their shareholders, the American public, to protect them, their borders, or their civilization from invasion and destruction.

They are playing at their "jobs," reaping the benefits without providing that which they each took an oath to provide. They are spending their paid time traveling and making speeches because this is much easier than taking care of the business of America, and it is much more profitable from a fundraising point of view. They think their job is to ensure they will have the resources to stay in power, rather than to work for those who hired them.

***

As previously stated and proven by these hack Presidents; the U.S.

Government is no longer government *"of the people, by the people, for the people."* It is more like Mexico's government of the oligarchy, for the oligarchy. Maybe this is the reason U.S. Presidents feel such a kinship with their Mexican counterparts rather than with the American people (?)

The U.S. Government is a bankrupt, corrupt and incompetent institution in every way, including morally as proven by Obama Administration personnel during the 2016 elections

Since the Mexican actions should have, long ago, ended any debate about putting the military on the U.S. border with Mexico, but this has not been done, nor has the media bothered to inform the American public about this, what is afoot?

Official agents of the government of Mexico have gotten away with attempted murder of American citizen agents of the U.S. Government and with, at the same time, promoting the illegal invasion of millions of their country's citizens into the United States. Is there a connection?

<u>Article I., Section 2. of the U.S. Constitution states:</u> ***<u>"Privilege of the writ of Habeas Corpus shall not be suspended, unless when in cases of Rebellion or Invasion the public safety may require it."</u>***

Note: Mexican government agents and military crossing the U.S. border and shooting at Americans represents ***"Invasion,"*** and endangering the ***"public safety"*** of at least some Americans. And also note the Constitution does not place any quantitative qualifier of how many citizens' ***"safety"*** put at risk ***"may require it."***

The intention of ***"the writ of Habeas Corpus"*** is to prevent, or correct, violations of personal liberty by directing judicial inquiry into the legality of detention. The supporters of illegal immigration have taken the position the illegal aliens cannot be detained because, after they are on U.S. soil, they have the same rights as American citizens, including *Habeas Corpus*.

Therefore, they cannot be detained, which is idiotic, given the *prima facie* evidence they have committed a crime is their very presence on U.S. soil.

The connection between ignoring the *"invasions"* and attacks upon Americans by not acting under Article I., Section 8.of the Constitution to call *"forth the Militia to ... repel"* these *"invasions,"* and Article I. Section 2., *"the writ of Habeas Corpus,"* is that action under the former would appropriately define the *"invasions"* for what they are, and trigger the latter. The *"Privilege of the writ of Habeas Corpus"* could be *"suspended."*

<u>In other words, should the President and U.S. Government do what they have the responsibility to do, protect the U.S., its property and its citizen's *"public safety,"* in accord with the U.S. Constitution, the nonsense argument of illegal alien immigrant's having the same "rights" as citizens would be moot! The illegal aliens could be stopped, rounded up and detained, which they should be anyway, because illegal entry IS breaking the law</u>

But this is just another case where the U.S. Government demonstrated its bias against American citizens. Although it has unconstitutionally violated the constitutionally provided protection of the Writ of *Habeas Corpus* of an American citizen, it refuses to do its duty when it applies to other than American citizens.

Given those in power in the U.S. Government must be cognizant of these facts, they are willfully not acting under the Constitution in the best interests of Americans. It is obvious they are not working for Americans but *"the Establishment"* that put them in power.

They are demonstrably willing to sacrifice America to fulfill the plans of a higher power. And that "power" has nothing to do with religion. It is the same power Jimmy Carter was satisfying by giving away the Panama Canal. They are stealth *New World Order* worker bees. There is no other logical explanation.

***

If the intent of seekers of refuge from capitalism populating the U.S. Government is the stealthy fulfilling of *New World Order*, One World Government plans to stay in power in the U.S. Executive, Don Meredith will be needed sooner rather than later to sing "America's" new theme song, *"Turn Out the Lights, the Party's Over."*

The Latino population will reach the critical mass of population to take over parts of the U.S. and representation in Congress to the extent they will redefine whole areas of America with their Latin culture, turning it into a replication of Mexico, poverty and all.

Their population is already reaching a point in some states wherein Latino *"pride"* is beginning to affect business and politics in that the Spanish language, Latin culture and politics are displacing English, American culture and values. They do not have to speak English because their population is such a large percentage of the population they only have to speak to one another, and they are too uneducated to understand the value of English to them.

There has already been a case, in 2002, in Florida, of a white, native born, English speaking American citizen being fired from her state government job because of her failure to speak Spanish. God help us because it seems earthly intervention is unavailable!

"The Establishment" media nonsense about Mexican contribution of cheap immigrant labor being necessary to the American farming industry is another negative.

European farming is being modernized to be technically superior while the U.S., which has been the superior producer for over one hundred years, is relying on cheap, Third World labor. Again, this will result in the U.S. heading directly for Third World status in an industry it has dominated for over a century.

What's wrong with those who support illegal immigration and make comments that they *"don't agree with"* those who have a position against "illegal" immigration? What kind of a mind does it take to disagree with being against something "illegal"? Wonder whether they disagree trespassing is illegal.

Don't they understand something that is "illegal" is against the law, and *"laws"* are one of the *"main foundations of every state,"* including the United States?

"Useful Idiot, liberal progressives" also like the idea of their position that the U.S. is an *"immigrant nation,"* therefore, Mexican immigration is in the American tradition and is *"good."*

This overlooks the fact America's immigrant success has been the result of legal immigration <u>and assimilation</u> wherein the immigrants and their children have joined American mainstream culture and learned to speak the language without the necessity to forget their Irish, Italian, or other heritages.

But they were mostly Europeans with the same values that built first world Europe and North America, not Latin Third World steeped in their religion and language because they have done nothing to be proud of during the past six hundred years the first world has passed them by. Don't believe this? Spend some time around a cathedral in Mexico.

This is not what is wrong with the Mexicans. They are displacing American culture and its more efficient language with their own backward language and culture out of *"pride"* that is being encouraged by the *"liberal, progressives"* in order to further the success of their "*divide and conquer.*"

This does not bode well for the future of America. It indicates the new, Latin immigrant population, unlike the European immigrant population, is ignorant of the benefits of the culture and language to which they are coming to escape the bonds of their own culture with which they ignorantly desire to displace ours, and within which they ignorantly desire to remain. They are bringing their culture and language with them to the detriment of <u>all</u> Americans and their country.

That the Mexicans immigrating to the U.S. even have *"pride"* in Latin, or Mexican culture, when compared to Western culture, and desire to speak Spanish, rather than English, is further demonstration of an ignorance that does not hold a promising future for an America with a large Latino population.

A pragmatic look at the world at the beginning of the 21st Century should cause anyone who is intelligent to have something less than *"pride"* in either the Spanish language, or the Mexican, or Latin cultures.

***

A realistic look at the world of the Spanish language versus English, and the Protestant world versus the world of the Latin Church would provide an objective, intelligent person with all the necessary information needed to show the benefits of English and Western culture over Spanish and Latin culture.

In 1992, the average per capita GDP of the three hundred million Spanish-speaking people of the world was about twelve hundred U.S. dollars, while the average per capita GDP of the three hundred sixty million people whose first language is English was twenty three thousand dollars, twenty times greater.

Thus the Spanish language is demonstrably the language of poverty, whereas the English language is the language of wealth.

The average per capita GDP of the four hundred million members of the Latin Church, including the populations of Spain and Italy, was sixty four hundred dollars, while the average per capita GDP of the nine hundred million members of Protestant churches, including Russia and the Ukraine which were under the constraints of Communism for seventy years, and South Africa, was seventeen thousand dollars.

If Russia, the Ukraine and South Africa were excluded the per capita GDP of Western Protestants was twenty-two thousand dollars. Therefore, given either the best, or the worst case, the per capita GDP of Protestants was three to four times greater.

Thus the culture of the Latin Church is also demonstrably a culture of poverty relative to the culture of the Protestant Church that is a culture of wealth.

However, it is not necessary for anyone to change his religion to become a participant in the benefits of the Western culture. There are many Catholics and practitioners of other religions in America who are very successful. But English is mandatory for anyone desiring to contribute to the American economy and realize the American dream benefits thereof.

There are more people in the world whose first language is English than there are whose first language is Spanish. More important is the fact that English has the most widespread use of any language.

Almost six hundred million people have elected English as a second language, resulting in a total worldwide English-speaking population of almost one billion people, almost three times as many people as the number that communicate in Spanish.

For Mexican immigrants to persist in speaking Spanish out of *"pride"* is ludicrous, especially when those people from much more successful cultures and countries such as Germans, Italians, Scandinavians, and others who having immigrated to the U.S. adopted English in order to be more successful. "When in Rome" is a concept with which the most intelligent abide.

Continuing to indulge in the characteristics of their Latin culture and speak Spanish, thereby depriving themselves of fully participating in the superior benefits of America's Western culture out of *"pride"* represents a Third World ignorance that cannot be enhancing to America. And given their proclivities, their increasing numbers, and their failure to adapt, it is perfectly fair to define their invasion of the U.S. in terms of a threat to the American system, American culture, and the American economy.

Note in the prior paragraph Latin and Western cultures are addressed…two different cultures inhabiting approximately the same spaces in America. But the fact is there are also African and Asian cultures represented in significant numbers.

But do we hear about this in the media? No. We hear, every day about the "*community*" when media and government representatives are addressing these two major groups that have reached critical mass. In each case what we are seeing and hearing is political correctness at work.

Both of these groups have cultural differences between one another, as well as differences with "Western culture" values regarding education, work ethic, religion, language, women versus men, etc., etc. because when any group becomes sufficiently large the members always seek the comfort of their culture.

Next time you hear about the "*community*," realize this means culture… as differentiated from America's majority western culture by political correctness.

It is probably with this knowledge the *New World Order* and "*the Establishment*" are extremely happy with the success of their pro-illegal Mexican immigration policies, and that successive U.S. Governments have continued the policies that were so successful under them by ignoring their duties under the U.S. Constitution to stop this alien invasion

If the American public were not being deprived of knowledge of what is going on at the Mexican border by the One World Government, pro-weakening of the U.S., elements of the media, they would probably be in full concurrence with the Mexican southern border policy, and demand the U.S. Government to act in accord with the U.S. Constitution to respond to the Mexican military incursions, and repel the invasion of illegal Mexican immigrants by suspending the Writ of *Habeas Corpus* as authorized in Article I of the U.S. Constitution, detaining and deporting them to secure the future of a non-Latin, democratic and prosperous United States.

After all, President Bush unconstitutionally suspended *Habeas Corpus* for the American citizen his Administration held in jail without counsel by declaring, *"He is where he ought to be."* Why not do it, legally, to protect Americans, as he and all U.S. Presidents swear to do at their Inaugurations, by putting the illegal Mexican immigrants back in Mexico where they *"ought to be"*?

***

The foregoing addresses *"the Establishment"* deliberately importing thousands of people from Third World countries, Cuba, Vietnam, Cambodia, Laos as well as encouraging and facilitating illegal immigration of millions from Mexico, and the organized distribution of these people around the country to ensure *their "divide and conquer"* program of *"diversity"* is established throughout America.

They also imported thousands from Somalia, Ethiopia and possibly other Third World Countries, and did the same distribution with them as part of this plan over the last two and one-half decades.

Obama even recently, blatantly did this… likely because the inflow from Mexico had recently been insufficient to keep their destruction plan on schedule.

"Blatantly" because this importation of tens of thousands of young children from Honduras, the only Central America country in which the U.S. Government has a large presence, including the military, was very well organized.

They were bussed two thousand miles across Mexico, ushered through immigration and disbursed in a way that demonstrated prior planning.

In addition to the tightly knit structure of Latin families never permitting their children to be exported from their country alone in this way, neither the children nor their families would have been able to organize or finance this operation that has the fingerprints of U.S. planning all over it.

Of course for each of the children at least two parents and other family members were not too far behind. So this brought hundreds of thousands more dependents of the same culture as Mexico into the country at a cost of billions of dollars to American taxpayers to have their communities and towns further diversified culturally for the benefit of *"the Establishment."* Brzezinski *NWO "Divide and Conquer"* plan.

Obama being the current titular head of the operational arm of the cabal of destruction we should understand why he did this. But it is impossible to fathom why he is doing what he was for the last several months of 2016 at the time of this writing, or why the choice of *"the Establishment"* to replace him vowed to increase this by over five hundred percent. Hopes of creating another Pearl Harbor-like event as they stated in advance of "9/11"?

This bringing into the U.S. by Obama of thousands of Muslim refugees from Syria and other Mid East locales from which radical Islamic terrorism is being spread after every one of his military and security advisors informed him these refugees would be infiltrated by potential terrorists. is an unconscionably heinous act on the part of this President whose multiplicity of Alinsky inspired and Brzezinski guided anti-American immigration and racially divisive acts over eight years had already done irreparable damage to the peace and harmony, and safety of all Americans.

And note: he brought almost five hundred of these potential terrorists into the U.S. during the week after the weekend terrorism in Orlando wherein fifty Americans were slaughtered by an Islamic Terrorist.

Also many more innocent Americans have needlessly died at the hands of those he and Bush refused to designate as *"Radical Islamic Terrorists."*

It is the writer's opinion we are too far past the time when he could mentally justify this with his mentor, Brzezinski's comment, *"There isn't a global Islam."* There is too much *"global"* evidence to negate this in any sane, rational mind.

So, we will have to leave this with the thought; immigration to *"diversify"* to *"divide and conquer"* is one thing, but aiding and abetting murder is quite another.

Therefore, whoever is responsible for bringing into the U.S. after the Orlando attack anyone who commits an attack resulting in the death of anyone should suffer the full extent of the law possible for aiding and abetting murder.

STEP FIVE: HEALTHCARE

IMPLEMENTING CONTROLS ON HEALTHCARE TO CONTROL THE PEOPLE AND CREATE A TOTALITARIAN STATE

1992, the year Bill Clinton was elected President, was almost two decades after Rockefeller and Brzezinski formalized their organization to enhance the power of the corporate/government *"Establishment."*

During this time their plans were being implemented and expanded to the detriment of ninety-nine percent of Americans and their country, as proven by the cost of housing being four times greater, private transportation three and one-third times greater, food three and one-half times greater, and the cost of healthcare more than five and one-half times greater.

The healthcare system during that time, and since, has been seriously, adversely affected and become exorbitantly expensive primarily as a result of the success of their plans to *"divide and conquer"* the population through immigration, as well as the success of Lyndon Johnson's *"Great Society."*

The explosion of Mexican immigration after Carter's signing of the Refugee Act of 1980, adding millions more to the population who could not afford to pay for their healthcare, and the planned breakup of black families through welfare legislation that turned a majority of the black population into welfare dependent single parent families added tremendously to the total cost of healthcare for all Americans.

The cost of providing this free healthcare to millions of non-paying, mostly impoverished recipients who procreate at a higher rate and require more healthcare than most citizens of America, has been laid off on average, responsible, working, asset owning, taxpaying Americans, driving up their costs while fewer of them are employed, and those who are have been losing purchasing power as a direct result of this and other actions of *"the Establishment"* in charge of the government.

Though it is not politically correct to talk about, the procreation rate of Mexican immigrants that is two to three times that of Protestant white America, seventy percent of black babies born out of wedlock, the cost of gang warfare gunshot victims, the quarter-million-dollar cost for each crack baby before they leave the hospital, etc. by people who are demonstrably less personally, socially and economically responsible are all laid on the backs of average, working, taxpaying Americans of all ethnic groups.

For example: before Johnson's *"Great Society"* average working, taxpaying Americans could go to the hospital and add a new member to their family for a total cost of less than one thousand dollars. But by 1992 they were charged an amount equal to the cost of seven babies to cover the cost of the non-payers.

Let's not forget this was not monetary inflation. It was population "inflation."

And on the subject of healthcare, let's put something to rest. That would be the years' long rhetorical debate about not having… and the non-desirability of… "Socialized medicine" in the U.S.

How would healthcare provided free to tens of millions by the Government, but paid for with funds taken from others be classified? What would this form of government be called?

The answer should be obvious to rational, intelligent, objective minds. So…..

***

In 1993, Bill Clinton's first year in office, presumably because of this unsustainable healthcare situation providing cover, Hillary Clinton attempted to impose her version of a stealth healthcare system on America she created illegally, out of public view.

It would have nationalized fifteen percent of the U.S. economy, rationed healthcare of Americans and turned over to Government bureaucrats, decisions who would receive what care.

This would have added to the size of the Government tremendously, in addition to removing legal protection under the law of *"physician/patient privilege."* Thus, actually changing the law, and reaching into the private lives of people as probably never done before… at least not in America.

Remember: Hillary was a lawyer at the time she proposed this. But she became a lawyer after passing the bar in Arkansas after failing the District of Columbia bar exam. So maybe in addition to not being licensed (unless she passed the D.C. bar exam later) she might not have been fully cognizant of the law.

But, as she has proven over and over since, "making false statements" to Federal Government investigators in 1996 and even as Secretary of State... which she treated like a worldwide traveling fellowship, visiting one hundred and twenty countries... deliberately breaking the laws regarding handling classified documents, committing perjury by lying to Congress and obstruction of justice in destroying evidence, she does not think laws apply to her.

So, additionally, she planned to criminalize the conduct of any Americans over the age of sixty-five who sought unapproved healthcare, or healthcare providers who provided any non-approved care to them.

She also planned to reduce the number of doctors by twenty-five percent and the number of specialists by fifty percent, virtually eliminating medical science advancement in the U.S.

Presumably this was to provide funding for the massive increase in Government employment required to intervene in every doctor/patient decision in America.

Her plan included a card be provided to each person that would be required for access to healthcare. This is reasonable and normal except for one little addition: her cards would be geographically limited, thus limiting people's movements unless they were willing to risk not having access to healthcare.

This was little different from Mao's China at the time wherein Chinese citizens and everyone else in the country was limited geographically by their "papers," which brings to mind the subject of immigration again.

What if America, since at least 1980, had a border crossing reciprocal arrangement with Mexico wherein it required all Americans and others who are not Mexican citizens to have government issued "papers" if they are in the country?

This is a fair question at this point because we are discussing a major problem created to a very great extent by Mexicans entering the U.S. without "papers."

After all, Bill Clinton and George Bush were friends with the President of Mexico, and familiar with the fact Americans caught in the country without proper "papers" would be treated exactly as Central Americans crossing Mexico's southern border: sent to jail!

Presumably both have a very different view than most Americans of what friendship is. But back to Hillary.

Why would she have desired to limit the travel of Americans within their own country on the ostensible basis of healthcare, yet at the same time be a *bona fide* member of "*the Establishment,*" supporting the mass "*migration*" of Mexicans traveling freely into, and within the U.S?

How would she have handled their healthcare? Would they have been given a pass on needing cards for their free healthcare, or assigned geographically limiting cards also. So many questions about an illogical plan that failed to address the cause and effect of the problems at hand: too many people not paying for their healthcare and how to pay for this?

It seems she was just too "hung up" on creating a Socialist Totalitarian state to be bothered with the actual problems, a position she was supported in from the very top of "*the* [destructive] *Establishment.*"

During the process of endeavoring to impose this destructive totalitarian program that would have been prohibitively expensive, as well as destroy much of what was "America" at that time before Obama, her husband, Bill the President, was brought into the discussion.

In an interview about the proposed program Bill suggested some of it might be flexible... subject to change. Subsequent to this Senator Jay Rockefeller, nephew of THE David Rockefeller, was told this by a member of the press.

His response, "*Well, he* [the President] *should ask his wife about that,*" tells us all we need to know. Hillary was a *bona fide* member of "*the Establishment*" close to the top ranks of its structure as far back as when she was at Yale in the early 1970s, as confirmed by her, since she claims to have met Bill at Yale.

In an interview after she was in the White House, in response to a question, she stated, "*My! I have known________ even longer than I have known my husband.*"

The person whose name is excluded here is a <u>very</u> powerful member of the unnamed "*Establishment,*" organization, close to its two founders, who the media never mentions, but has played a large role in many Government decisions over the years since

1973, and possibly before, as well as being a member of the boards of numerous major corporations in the list of *Members of the Club.*

Hillary is the best example alive in America today of the phrase *"Power corrupts, absolute power corrupts absolutely!"* She has been protected by the very powerful behind the U.S. Government for so long she has no problem lying under oath, or breaking any of the country's laws. She seems immune.

The Director of the FBI and the Attorney General of the U.S. proved this in July 2016. Don't expect her to change. She won't, and if she achieves her goal *"Turn out the Lights"* should definitely be the song to replace the national anthem.

Her history proves this *"absolutely!"*

But thankfully, she was not successful in this, her first totalitarian effort in imposing a "healthcare" program to control people on unsuspecting Americans at that time.

Since then the inflation in costs of living continued to become much worse, especially in the case of healthcare, in which the Government has the most hand.

The increases in salary, wages and retirement benefits have not even come close to keeping up with the increases in living costs. Clearly, the programs of *"the Establishment"* have served only to impoverish Americans. But not to worry! The next *"Establishment"* whore to address the "health" care problems at least had a plan that solved the problem of "how to pay for this?"

***

LYING ABOUT "HEALTH" INSURANCE AND FORCING THOSE WITH ASSETS TO FATTEN INSURANCE COMPANY COFFERS

In 2008, it was time for Barrack Obama to take a crack at doing what Hillary failed to do on behalf of the Rockefeller/Brzezinski *"Establishment"* while also following Alinsky's guidance to wreak as much damage on "America" as humanly possible in eight years, guiding it into the history dustbin of failed Socialist states.

At this point we should remember their influence on Obama. So, not surprisingly Barrack decided immediately to hang his legacy on "healthcare," and pushed his vision of "healthcare" reform that satisfies Rockefeller and Brzezinski's Plan for America through Congress a decade and a half after Hillary's was shot down.

He did this with knowledge it has "squat" to do with healthcare, and he was lying to Americans all the time he was further impoverishing them while enriching insurance company executives.

He deliberately increased the costs of already insured working, asset holding Americans by increasing by fifty to one hundred percent their cost of "health" insurance, and getting young Americans who do not need it to pay for it through unconstitutional penalties, complements of *"the Establishment"* Supreme Chief Justice installed by the second Bush.

Why would he do this only so these billions and billions of dollars… eventually amounting to trillions if America can stand that long after what Obama and his two predecessors have done… can be unnecessarily taken from working, taxpaying Americans and passed through insurance companies when he is fully aware there is no such thing as "health" insurance?

We should, by now, know the answer to that, but to ensure everyone understands the *"Why?"* part of it, let's explain what Obama knew about "there is no such thing as 'health' insurance."

He knew insurance was not required for people to obtain healthcare because it is legislated hospitals cannot turn away those in need of it if they cannot pay.

He also knew because he was a community organizer; all the costs of uninsured care for inner city gunshot, and accident victims and any other healthcare, including births of the exploding populations of illegal immigrants and other inner city populations were already covered by working Americans and companies through income tax payments.

He had to know this because informing his inner city clients of this was part of his only pre-political paying employment as a community organizer

He also knew, as do the non-paying recipients; <u>"health insurance" is not required for them to receive care because they do not possess assets against which healthcare providers can place liens to collect their exorbitant fees,</u> which are primarily the result of their having to "eat" the costs of providing for the non-payers that are not reimbursed by the Government.

He was probably also aware the major cause of bankruptcy filings of most retired Americans is they have only as much insurance as they can afford, which is frequently insufficient to cover the exorbitant costs of their healthcare that is a result of the non-paying minority patients like his community organizer clients.

But that was obviously not a concern for him. Other Americans are not his clients.

He proved this when he provided free cell phones and time to inner city residents. But did not provide them to any other Americans.

Obama and all others in the Government are aware of its inability to cover the cost of all those who do not pay. Its current and anticipated taxation revenue stream covers barely half of the current cost of his greatly expanded government.

As well as this tremendous current cost, he is deliberately increasing costs through "*the Establishment*" "*divide and conquer*" plans by planning for those already here illegally to become voters, and planning even more to follow to further enhance governmental power… and increase costs.

He is also aware taxes on corporations already the highest in the industrialized world cannot be increased nor would further tax increases on the working be politically acceptable even though that is from whence he and his socialist, actually communist, Government cronies know the money must come.

Therefore, although Obama knows "there is no such thing as health insurance" because he knows it is only asset protection insurance he could not refer to it by this true name without informing the ignorant masses they do not require what he, a modern sort of snake oil salesman, desired to sell to them that they do not need without informing them of what he was really doing.

He knows Obamacare, AKA the Affordable Care Act, is nothing but a socialist redistribution of wealth through further taxation on those with assets who are already paying more than they can afford. So, rather than a tax, he presented it in a non-constitutional format of forced payments to "health" insurance companies that are now stripping out their further unnecessary share of the dwindling wealth of working Americans.

This is for being the middlemen to provide "insurance" coverage to welfare receiving members of the population who will continue to receive care free via subsidies provided at the expense of the now further burdened taxpayers through increases in the cost of their asset protection "health" insurance.

<u>Now, hopefully, every reader understands Obama is still nothing but a "community organizer" head of a national corporate/socialist regime working to equalize the wealth of his constituency base of non-working dependents with that of those who work and contribute, while diverting as much as he can from contributors into coffers of his second constituency of corporations and their executives who in turn reward him and other seekers of refuge from capitalism, its risk and work requirements by hiding out in Government, or as lobbyists.</u>

He is doing the same as all his predecessors since Carter, except Reagan; pursuing conversion of the U.S. from an ostensibly representative democracy to a plutocratic, centrally controlled, corporate/government Socialist, Totalitarian State as promulgated by his *"outstanding thinker"* mentor, Zbigniew Brzezinski.

He is also rewarding international corporations that already benefit from not paying taxes on foreign income kept overseas with even more profits potentially to be kept tax free through accounting treatments involving overseas divisions while being rewarded lavishly for this and keeping Americans ignorant all this is at their expense, not knowing what is being done to them and unaware to thwart their demise what they need do is follow and stop the M-O-N-E-Y they should be aware is the problem, considering Obama like the Clintons had very little before entering the Presidency after almost eight years of earning only three hundred thousand a year in 2016 has a reported net worth of over nine million dollars. (He must have been trading cattle futures.)

He probably also knew his "health" insurance plan would also assist him in lies about the economy. The way GDP, Gross Domestic Product, is calculated the massive increased costs of his plan paid by taxpaying Americans actually increased the reported GDP, helping cover up some of his real economic destruction.

Meanwhile, not a damned thing about actual physical healthcare has changed except it costs twice as much as it did before Obamacare, and it seems to have become more limited, especially to older, retired Americans on that "entitlement" called Medicare they paid into for forty years, and do not have the choice to cease paying more into each month until they die.

Obviously we now know Hillary and Obama's Totalitarian programs are structured not to solve any of the problems plaguing Americans because they were deliberately created to change America, as Obama promised at the beginning of his reign. He just failed to reveal the changes would be to worsen our plight.

All he did in this example was transfer some of the wealth of working, contributing, asset-owning taxpayers to two of his real constituencies: 1.) non-working, inner-city, welfare-receiving, Government dependents, many of whom have never worked a day in their life, and 2.) insurance companies and their executives who will be able to pay back much of their Obama generated largesse to their America destroying *Establishment*" cohorts who can now use their new "found money" to wreak further damage on us, our lifestyles and our country.

STEP SIX: GUN CONTROL

REMOVE THE ABILITY TO DEFEND THEMSELVES FROM THE GOVERNMENT TO CREATE A POLICE STATE.

Note: *"THEMSELVES"* refers to the people of America in which *"the Establishment"* have been working assiduously since 1973 *"TO CREATE A POLICE STATE"* in America.

These are frightening words we know Hillary Clinton and Barrack Obama have followed since they were college students. It appears both must have been adherents of ideas that were the guidepost for *"leftist counter-culture"* that was opposed to the American culture. They were radicals in their young adulthood.

Then throughout their adult political lives both have proven through actions and statements they bought into, and have endeavored to implement policies of population control.

If many members of the electorate were aware in the 1980s and 1990s what these two were interested in doing to America neither would have had political careers unless they emigrated to Eastern Europe.

Thus the dishonest, *"leftist Establishment""* U.S. media in which many had to have known about these two could have saved America from the destruction both wrought.

But what is even more frightening is since the major players in *"the Establishment"* have supported and promoted these two for decades this informs us what those in control of our Government were still pursuing for Americans via Hillary for President.

On this subject of *"gun control"* it is obvious what Hillary, Barrack and others in *"the Establishment"* in control of the U.S. Government and all the *"leftist"* media advocates for *"gun control"* really want to do to America.

They want to remove our ability to protect ourselves from them as they turn America into a non-sovereign, borderless, *"leftist"* Police State member of their *New World Order* modeled on Stalin's USSR.

This is pure evil! There is no other word for it. Hillary Clinton, Barrack Obama, Zbigniew Brzezinski and all the others in *"the Establishment,"* controlled media and the Government advocating and working to implement this and the other five steps to destroy America are pure evil incarnate!

Hillary Clinton and Barrack Obama are the faces of the evil pursuing the destruction of the "America" most Americans and the world loved. <u>It is time they need to be shown to the electorate what they really are</u>.

***

Since Hillary was raising the issue of Trump's tax returns, there should be a big push on the part of the Trump campaign to get her to unseal and grant public access to her college thesis, all her speeches to *"the Establishment"* and all others, in addition to all her Emails, including those her State and "Justice" Department co-conspirators are endeavoring to withhold until after the election for reasons that should be obvious.

Given she insists all these contain no *"Classified"* information and the State Department amazingly concurs, stating they will release them, they are defined public information, and must be released before the election… if this country has not already become a totalitarian regime under control of a Clinton, Obama cabal! (A year plus later this appears the case.)

She is already disliked. If the public is made aware of her thinking and what she has been working to do to America for the last forty years she would be "toast."

"Crooked Hillary" is one thing, but *"**America destroying Hillary"*** is another.

Most people think there are crooks everywhere, especially in Government. But they don't associate this with any adverse effect on them personally. However, they do relate to America and understand what destroying it would do to them personally, which is important.

"America destroying" personalizes it for everyone. Thus, this would be "partisan for America."

***

Amendment II. of the Constitution of the United States states, *"… **the right of the people to keep and bear Arms, shall not be infringed.**"*

This is a complete thought, and it is obvious the first part of this Amendment, *"A well-regulated Militia, being necessary to the security of a free State…"* was intended to be made up of *"the people"* with *"Arms"* to maintain the *"security of a free State."*

Amendment IX. States, *"The enumeration in the Constitution, of certain rights, shall not be construed to deny or disparage others retained by the people."*

Therefore, *"A well-regulated Militia"* cannot, in any legitimate way, *"be construed to deny"* that *"the right of the people to keep and bear Arms"* is granted, or *"enumerated,"* elsewhere in the Constitution.

In this year of 2016, this *"right"* of individuals, *"the people,"* to own firearms, *"arms,"* is one with which most legal scholars concur. It is still argued, however, by the *"liberal,"* and gun control advocates, especially in media such as THE NEW YORK TIMES Op Ed columns, that the Constitution confers the right to bear arms only upon a *"Militia,"* and not upon the citizens.

Constitutional "Right" Confirmed

To his credit, Attorney General, John Ashcroft stated a decade ago, ***"Let me state unequivocally my view that the text and the original intent of the Second Amendment clearly protect the right of individuals to keep and bear firearms. While some have argued that the Second Amendment guarantees only a 'collective right' of the states to maintain militias, I believe the amendment's plain meaning and original intent prove otherwise."***

Further, the Ashcroft Justice Department, unlike what we have had for the last eight years, defended gun laws. His department's stated position was, *"...the Second Amendment more broadly protects the right of individuals, including persons who are not members of any militia or engaged in active military service or training, to possess and bear their own firearms, subject to reasonable restrictions designed to prevent possession by unfit persons or to restrict the possession of types of firearms that are particularly suited to criminal misuse."*

Given this Attorney General's statement and that of his Justice Department, it would seem the Bush Administration was on the side of the people regarding the right to bear arms. But, as usual, there was some ambivalence. And this is a fair assessment given the cabinet level positions of those, both of whom reported directly to the President. Problem is; the Clinton and Obama Administrations both assiduously pursued destruction of the people's rights.

Continuum of "Establishment" Control

Secretary of State, Colin Powell's office supported a position that could explain why he was advanced over many others to his high military position. That was his ridiculously anti-American position the United States should sign a United Nations gun control treaty.

Given the United Nations has a stated objective of disarming the entire world, especially the U.S., except for itself in the form of its military that would be the control element of its *New World Order* One World Government, why did not the Bush Administration disavow the Powell position and have a consistent policy for both domestic and foreign dissemination?

This lack of a clearly defined policy on this issue so important to the freedom of Americans is disconcerting, but not surprising because the little Bush was a strictly *NWO* President following in his father's footsteps on every issue.

However, the knowledge that at least some members of that administration were on the side of the American public should give Americans comfort relative to the position of the previous, "*liberal*," Clinton Administration and the even more so Obama Administration that have consistent policy on the issue.

The entire Clinton Administration was with Hillary on the side of the United Nations in its desire to disarm honest, law-abiding, Americans… as she still is.

Notable among "*the Establishment*" members of the Clinton Administration in the anti-gun ownership corner was the Vice President, Al Gore, who, it should be noted, did beat Bush in the popular vote of the ignorant American electorate.

This is important because if it were not for the fact the citizens of Gore's home state of Tennessee voted for Bush, Gore would have been President, and the administration that would have been in power in 2001 would have aggressively moved the U.S. in the direction of the United Nations on this issue as well as many others in conflict with the interests of Americans… as has Obama.

The people of Tennessee elected not to support their native son because they knew him and his position on the issue of gun control. Many others probably voted for him because they really did not know him. Otherwise, the degree of concurrence with "the *liberal Establishment*" of the American electorate bodes very badly for the future of freedom, as does the fact that "*Establishment*" President Bush signed the Campaign Reform Act unconstitutionally restricting groups such as the National Rifle Association from running advertising sixty days prior to elections to inform and educate the voters during the time it is really important to do so.

The fact the Bush II Administration chose not support the Ashcroft position but that of Clinton and Obama demonstrates the fact of the "two party" sham perpetrated on Americans, as well as the pro United Nations, One World Government position of Bush.

Gun Control "Establishment"

The position of so-called "*liberals*" like Hillary and Obama regarding the right of citizens to bear arms has been well articulated for years. They have been strongly in favor of limiting through "*gun control*" the individual's right to bear arms.

This "*Establishment*" position has not changed. But rather than continuing to openly inform voters of their true intent, after the Gore loss in Tennessee, they... at least for a while, surely to Hillary's dismay... tempered their official policy to a more broadly acceptable "*sensible gun safety.*" However since Obama they flipped back to "*control,*" which, thankfully, helped make candidate Hillary a less viable candidate.

This will be more difficult to address from an opposition point of view should Republicans endeavor to support the positions of those members of the electorate they purport to represent.

The "*liberal*" position on gun control has never made much sense. It seems illogical for anyone to desire to deprive himself of the right to protect his family and property, by suppressing the rights of everyone to own a gun.

Surely, there cannot be many who count themselves in the "*liberal*" camp who do not understand the meaning of the term "outlaw" even if they don't understand the term "criminal."

Obviously, both terms describe those who choose not to abide by the laws most members of society abide by. Thus, by definition, criminals choosing to ignore the law would still have guns, while the law-abiding would not have the means to protect against them.

Still, members of "*the Establishment*" its media and the Hollywood *"liberal"* contingent assiduously pursue the disarmament of American citizens. They do this while they must be fully aware of the very large criminal element that would surely be a threat to many of them who have obvious wealth, demonstrated in the size and locations of their homes and their expensive automobiles.

For example: The *"liberal"* Hollywood supporters of *"gun control"* (and Clinton/Obama) could not live in Los Angeles without being aware of the very large criminal element versus the meager police resources.

They could not be unaware of the estimated twenty thousand armed gang members (outlaws and criminals) residing within an easy fifteen minute drive of their large homes and families, or of the frequent home invasion robberies, car-jackings, and other crime in their city to which they are not immune. Why would these people advocate a position that could clearly be potentially so detrimental to their own health and safety?

The answer to this question has to be much like the answer to the query of why anyone would desire to be a Communist. The answer to that imponderable turned out to be quite simple. It was; the advocates of Communism… like Hillary and Obama, et al… are those who desire to be in charge.

The precepts of their desired "*leftist*" totalitarian society would not apply to them. They would be the enforcers of the precepts. Just as in Hillary Clinton's Totalitarian Socialist scheme to ration healthcare of Americans wherein she was never concerned her healthcare would be rationed because she envisioned herself as the one who would be doing the rationing.

The Clintonesque, *"liberal,"* advocates of "gun control" would never have their guns "controlled." Their positions would exempt them, and they would still have the means to protect themselves, their property and their families. Only the majority, the proletariat of their utopian society, would be left to fend for themselves minus the benefit of the right to bear arms.

Should anyone not believe this the case, consider the following: Sarah Brady who for the last thirty years has been one of the leading, most vociferous, politically connected and media supported, voices of the *"gun control"* element, preaching the evil of guns, and the removal of them from the hands of Americans, gave HER son a rifle for a Christmas present.

Further, television "personality" and avidly aggressive, anti-gun proponent, Rosie O'Donnell, who frequently used her television program as a platform from which to spout her rabid, *"liberal, progressive Establishment"* agenda, including the elimination of guns, had her personal body guard apply for a concealed weapon permit for her protection.

Let's not forget the Socialist (Democrat) veneer of the *faux* "two party" system. Even though their position is avid *"gun control,"* their congressional members have had hunting fundraisers. Yes, that is "hunting" with a gun.

If anyone who is now aware of the true nature of "the *liberal Establishment gun control"* element cannot spell HYPOCRISY, they better be able to know the meaning of "elitist," actually *"effete elitist"* and what they believe.

That is, *"It's OK for me, but not for everyone else. I am in charge"* totalitarian thinking, because this is the way the Gores, Clintons, O'Donnells, Bradys, Obamas, even Bushes, "Hollywood," most of *"the Establishment"* and many others of their club who desire to deprive Americans of their rights and freedoms "think."

They are dangerous to the health, wealth and safety of all Americans!

Oxy"morons"!

As in their other positions, the *"liberal Establishment"* advocation of *"gun control"* is void of common sense, or any reliance on historical or contemporary evidence. In fact, their positions defy common sense and empirical evidence.

With complete disregard of the evidence of recidivism among sexual criminals, they promote leniency of incarceration. With one hundred percent of the evidence of human conduct to the contrary they promote *"diversity is strength."* With decades of evidence of the abysmal failure of wasteful Government programs such as the anti-poverty efforts, they continually seek more money for them. With the obvious disintegration of the fabric of American culture, and with it the productivity and standard of living of all Americans, they continue to insist on immigration programs that favor only those who cannot contribute to an increase in U.S. productivity. In fact, they work assiduously to inhibit immigration of those who could enhance technological advancement and productivity.

It is just not reasonable to assume so many, particularly those who are considered the "elite" of the *"liberal"* side of politics, could be so unaware of the facts of quantifiable failures, criminal recidivism, the empirically evident conduct of humans, or of the impact of Third World immigration. They, the *"elite"* cleric, are given credit for much more intellectual acuity than their ridiculous positions indicate they possess.

Now, the majority of *"liberal*s," those in the congregation, are different. When one of them takes a position like: *"You must have a license and register a car, so you should have to register a gun and have a license to own one."* You endeavor to show to them the fallacy of their "thinking" by pointing out it is legal to own a car without registration or licensing. These are required only if the car is placed into operation on public streets.

Similar laws for guns already exist because licenses are required for hunting, or should anyone want to actually carry a gun. If their eyes begin to glaze over, or there is some other indication they are incapable of coping with facts, or these simple concepts, you can be assured you are addressing a member of the congregation of *"liberal*ism" for whom *"gun control"* is just part of the dogma.

Since the *"liberal"* clerics like Hillary and Obama must be given credit for fully understanding the eventual ramifications on America and its citizens of the positions with which they are indoctrinating the minds of their congregation, and disseminating through the Government "school"/indoctrination system, their positions such as *"gun control"* deserve critical scrutiny.

Facts of Freedom

Machiavelli observed five hundred years ago *"The Swiss are strongly armed and completely free."*

This remains true in 2016. The Swiss are still strongly armed and completely free. And it was the Swiss who were the model for the American Democratic Republic. The Swiss have not changed in over five hundred years.

All males in Switzerland are subject to some form of military service and training until the age of forty-two, and they take their military weapons home with them.

<u>Given the empirical evidence of Swiss success, it is intellectually difficult to cope with "reasoning" behind the persistence of supposedly intelligent people in their efforts to disarm honest, law-abiding citizens. There must be some sinister "evil" afloat in these efforts. There is not another intellectually reasonable explanation.</u>

Therefore, all Americans should be cognizant of the fact *"the liberal leftist Establishment"* do not acknowledge the existence of empirical evidence refuting their claims about guns, and they do so to prevent average Americans from being aware of such truths as the Swiss experience or the following:

-In some counties in the U.S., laws regarding the issuance of concealed weapon carrying permits have been loosened, making this privilege more readily available to the citizenry. The result: a decline in crime.

-In Australia, the government did what *"gun control"* advocates are endeavoring to do in America. They outlawed private ownership of guns: the crime rate soared.

-In the United Kingdom they have the most rigid gun restrictions in Europe, and, yes, you guessed it: they have the highest crime rates in Europe.

-Washington D.C. and Chicago have some of the strictest gun control laws in the U.S. They also have the highest murder rates. Surely there is some reason for this other than gun ownership. Possibly the demographic similarities between Washington and Chicago should be explored as a reason for the violence?

-In France, prior to the German invasion in World War II, gun owners were required to register their firearms with the local city government. The result: when the Germans invaded, they just went around collecting all of the registered guns, depriving the French of the opportunity to defend themselves.

It is this last point that is most salient in the minds of Hillary, Obama and other *"Establishment"* gun control totalitarians desiring to disarm Americans.

There is probably not a *"liberal"* alive who, in addition to being a *"gun control"* fanatic, is not also, either clerically consciously, or congregationally unconsciously, a strong supporter of "Big Government," a United Nations led *New World Order* One World Government, the Paris Climate Accord, NAFTA, the myth of "free trade," Globalism, larger foreign "aid" packages, higher taxes on the working, more welfare, or the many other foolish, oxymoronic non-common sense, internationalist and utterly intellectually insulting and mostly intellectually impossible, Utopian schemes to which an armed American citizenry presents a potential deterrence.

Need for Vigilance

Even without declared *"Liberals"* in office Americans who cherish their freedoms and the "rights" granted to them under the *Constitution of the United States*, should be ever vigilant of *"the Establishment."*

Bush II tied the hands of the National Rifle Association to prevent them from advertising to inform the public about those politicians who would deprive Americans of their *"right"* to bear arms during the last, important sixty days of election periods through his signing of the unconstitutional Campaign Reform Act.

This emboldened *"gun control"* advocates like Hillary, Obama and obviously Bush.

The Government, under the Bush Administration, clearly stated it would not use profiling to protect American lives against terrorism from male Islamic, non-citizen terrorists of Middle Eastern heritage between the ages of eighteen and forty.

Obama actions, including censoring Government use of the term *"Radical Islamic terrorists"* and deliberately importing potential terrorists seems eerily consistent with the Bush mindset.

Fact is; the Bush family, Hillary, Obama, Kristol, Romney and so many others unknown to the public are top members of each of the veneers of the one big *"Establishment"* party that has two thin publicly presented veneers.

This is the Reason Romney, along with many other Republicans, did everything within his empty suit personage to prevent Trump from being the Republican Presidential nominee, and the Bushes refused to support him.

Trump and any other non-*"Establishment"* person seeking any position of power is a threat to their many decades and generations of control that has enriched all of them... and not only do they not like it, will likely continue to do everything they can to keep their gravy train from being derailed.

Americans can bank on the fact their Government will, in the event of potentially devastating attacks against citizens by persons of this demographic, take every action within its power, whether legal or not, under cover of the "War," to prevent even the possibility of Americans possessing registered weapons defending themselves.

Machiavelli was an astute observer of human nature. He had a lot to say about the wisdom of people being armed. In the ensuing five hundred years, human nature has not changed, nor has the nature of those humans in positions of government power.

The nature of the source of conflicts also remains unchanged. Therefore, in the current atmosphere of the very strong, *"liberal,"* movement, even among Republicans, toward an increasingly, larger, more powerful government, and the Islamic Crusade against Western Culture, those who are interested in maintaining their Constitutional *"right"* to bear arms would be wise to seek Machiavellian pragmatic consultation:

"All armed prophets have conquered, and unarmed prophets have come to grief." - Machiavelli

"One should read history to discover the reasons for victories and defeats so he can avoid the latter and imitate the former."
- William Cowper

EPILOGUE

"The age of virtuous politics is past, and we are deep in that of cold pretense. Patriots are grown too shrewd to be sincere: and we are too wise to trust them." - William Cowper

Americans today are suffering *"The Establishment"* and government *"leftist, liberal progressive evils"* and their political correctness intended to prevent discussion of them. These "evils" are, in part:

- Deliberately created racial division designed, i.e., *"diversity"* through immigration to provide a *"liberal progressive"* power base at the expense of <u>all</u> Americans, and create a need for a larger, more Socialist Government.

-Gun control efforts to disarm law-abiding, honest Americans.

-A deplorable "education"/indoctrination system that, primarily as a result of *"diversity is strength"* multiculturalism, is the worst and most expensive in the Western world.

-An exorbitantly expensive healthcare system resulting primarily from the cost of providing free healthcare to all the Third World residents of America, and Mexican Nationals who do not pay for any of their healthcare.

-A U.S. Government, both "Socialist" Democrat and Republican, that pays taxpayer money to support a Socialist United Nations run by Third World, un-elected bureaucrats who have a plan to tax and disarm Americans, eliminate ownership of private property that is the cornerstone of democracy, and place everyone under a United Nations led, *New World Order,* One World Government.

AND many in *"the Establishment"* are also destroying many of American's freedoms, as well as endangering them.

Examples of this are:

-Drug "war" policies permitting unconstitutional invasions, and seizures of private property without proof of any crime.

-Continued conversion of the "education" system that was so important in providing America's prosperity into the Government indoctrination system.

-The U.S.A. Patriot's Act that deprived Americans, in one stroke of the pen under the dictates of political correctness of more rights and freedom than all previous administrations combined.

-The Transportation Safety Administration debacle with its thousands of federalized, unionized, non-terminable employees.

- Further economic destruction under more economy destroying trade deals.

- Potentially more Islamic terrorism.

- Creation of the Northern [military] Command for the United States, which signals the possibility of military on the streets of America.

This last one might be particularly troubling to all Americans given Presidential powers to declare a *"State of Emergency"* and rule under Executive Order.

Further, although it is not a pleasant thought, think what a U.S. President, as Commander in Chief, with the Totalitarian *"leftist"* One World Government leanings of one of the 2016 *"Establishment"* Presidential candidates desiring to disarm Americans would be able to do to the people with this force.

Also, given U.S. commitments to NATO and the United Nations, could these forces be far behind in "policing" the streets, and the citizens, of America?

These potential democracy depriving actions have been implemented by *"the Establishment,"* veneer Democrat and Republican alike, because there is no opposition from American citizens. They are banking on Americans being *"placidly governable"* and compliant. And based upon the evidence, it appears they are correct.

"Placidly governable," complacent Americans of today appear to possess the same mental and physical characteristics: they seem to be as intellectually lazy as they are physically lazy. And since that which they can see and feel does not seem to concern them, the perception is; the stealthy stealing of their rights, freedom, and their culture is also of no concern to them.

"...all experience hath shewn, that mankind are more disposed to suffer, while evils are sufferable, than to right themselves by abolishing the forms to which they are accustomed." -Thomas Jefferson

Declaration of Independence, July 4, 1776

This statement is just as true in 2016 as it was in 1776. In 1776 the suffering *"mankind"* of the American colonies decided to *"right themselves"* by casting off the bonds of the King of England.

Today, the question is: when are present-day Americans going to choose to peacefully *"right themselves"* as their ancestors did?

Donn W. Fletcher
July 18, 2016

Dear Reader,

Hopefully, reading this book was not necessarily a pleasant experience, but an informative learning experience which was the objective.

Knowledge is the foundation of freedom and democracy. That is the reason not much real knowledge is purveyed on the nation's TV monitors, in the schools or anywhere else. That is because knowledge is power!

If the majority of American people had knowledge of what was being done to them and their country by plan the last forty years they would have had the power to stop it. That is why they have deliberately been deprived of that knowledge.

Remember: Hitler could not have done what he did to Germany and the rest of Europe if not for his "information" minister Goebbels.

Therefore, think how different the world might be had these two men not been in control of what was presented in the media and what children learned in school, limiting what the people knew.

Although not a pleasant thought, this is relevant if you think about what has happened to American education, industry and productivity, the expansion of the Government into every aspect of our lives, the actual economic decline we have experienced while the Government continually lies about everything because they know those under forty do not have knowledge of the past to compare with today.

Control "education" of the youth and you control history by rewriting not only it but the present. This is where we are in 2016.

If we do not take control of the present to stop the lies, indoctrination and economic destruction of America to "level the playing field" by reducing our level of knowledge, productive capacity and overall wellbeing by those more interested in expanding their power and control America is literally "done."

As stated in financial publication Casey Research, *"All countries have a shelf life."* Also, everything has a life cycle represented by a bell shaped curve.

If we consider the *"shelf"* to be the bottom of the page at which the curve begins on the left and ends on the right, America is much closer to the bottom of the page on the right than it would be if not for those in control of us for the last forty years.

If America is not to crash prematurely into the *"shelf"* on the right side, prematurely ending the greatest experience of freedom and democracy humanity has ever known, we MUST *"throw 'the Establishment' bums out"* <u>now</u> to stop the carnage of America.

If we do not do this we will be the ones *FOR WHOM THE BELL TOLLS.* 2016 is our last opportunity to do this… ever!

Regards and thank you for reading,

Donn W. Fletcher
July 18, 2016

ABOUT THE AUTHOR

A one-year college dropout with a Master in Business Administration Degree from the Harvard University Graduate School of Business he spent the past sixty plus years experiencing the world in a diversity of ways, some by choice, some not.

He worked construction, was an enlisted man, Non-Commissioned and Commissioned Officer and staff member of a prestigious U.S. military school, small business owner, held multiple executive management positions, including Chief Operating Officer and board member of a NYSE company at the age of thirty-four, conducted business in North America, Australia where he started a company, Europe where he also lived, and Asia, including the Philippines, Japan, Taiwan and the People's Republic of China.

These adventures, plus experience and successes in consulting and management in marketing, retailing, construction and the entertainment industry, investing in real estate, and a little fun along the way, resulted in his experiencing the world as most Americans never do.